Acting in the
Million Dollar Minute

Acting in the
Million Dollar Minute

The Sequel

by Tom Logan

Anderson, S.C.
AND

Limelight Editions

Published in 2005 by
   Limelight Editions (an imprint of Amadeus Press, LLC)
   512 Newark Pompton Turnpike
   Pompton Plains, New Jersey 07444, USA

For sales, please contact
   Limelight Editions
   c/o Hal Leonard Corp.
   7777 West Bluemound Road
   Milwaukee, Wisconsin 53213, USA
   Tel. 800-637-2852
   Fax 414-774-3259

Website: www.limelighteditions.com

Illustrations by Cliff Mott

Printed in the United States of America

Library of Congress Cataloging-in-Publication Data

Logan, Tom, 1953–
   Acting in the million dollar minute : the sequel / Tom Logan.—
   1st Limelight ed.
       p. cm.
   ISBN 0-87910-307-8 (pbk.)
   1. Television acting—Vocational guidance. 2. Television advertising—
   Vocational guidance. I. Title.
   PN1992.8.A3L6 2005
   791.4502'8'023—dc22
                                                        2005005873

This book is dedicated in loving memory to "other daddo,"
whom I miss very much,
and to my wonderful sons, Lear and Baron.

To Lear: It's so fulfilling to hear you say,
"I love you more,"
but to that I reply,
"That's impossible."

To Baron: With the love we have between us,
the "birdie" will never die.

Contents

Introduction   xi

CHAPTER 1: The Importance of Commercials   1

The Commercial "Type" — Show Me the Money — Commercials Are Big Business — The Importance of Commercials for the Actor — Do I Have to Move to Los Angeles or New York? — The Birthing Process of a Commercial — Crawling Around on the Floor Acting like a Lion — When Does the Audition Begin?

CHAPTER 2: The Slate   17

The Importance of the Slate   Hitting Your Mark — The Frame Lines — What We Look For in the Slate — Other Things We May Ask For in the Slate — Should You Slate "in Character"? — Glasses and Slating — Tail Slate/ End Slate

CHAPTER 3: The Top Four Complaints about Your Performance   43

Complaint Number 1: No Human Qualities — Complaint Number 2: No Personality — Complaint Number 3: No Warmth — Complaint Number 4: No Fun

CHAPTER 4: Commercial Dialogue   67

Types of Commercials — Commercial Styles — Analyzing the Script — Comedy versus Drama — One-Liners — Marking the Script — The Good News–Bad News Syndrome — Coloring the Words — Transitions — Asides — Pacing the

*Copy — Accents and Dialects — Cue Cards versus Scripts —
Speaking from the Script — Speaking from Cue Cards —
The Teleprompter — The Earprompter — Memorizing
the Script — After the Dialogue*

CHAPTER 5: Basic Commercial Acting Principles   103
*No More Drunken Polar Bears — The Banging-Your-Head-
against-the-Wall Method — Frame of Reference —
Observation — Research through Observation — Character
Objective — Memory Substitution — Backstory/Prelife*

CHAPTER 6: The Hero   121
*Mentioning the Product Name — Words That Put the Product
in Its Best Light — Handling the Product — Miming and
Props — Eating the Product*

CHAPTER 7: Why Most Multi-Person Auditions Don't Work   135
*Discussing the Scene in Advance — The Director's Role:
Fixing the Scene*

CHAPTER 8: Multi-Person Commercials   147
*Can an Acting Partner Ruin Your Performance? — Try to
Find Out in Advance Who Your Partner Is — Study All Parts
— The Separation Problem — Two-Person Slates — Slating
Chemistry — Who Really Tells the Message in a Scene? —
Reacting to Third Parties — Building a Physical Relationship
— Give the Director an Editable Scene — Listening —
The Importance of Partner Chemistry — Reading from Your
Partner's Script — Pacing the Scene with Another Actor
— Anticipating Your Partner*

CHAPTER 9: Openings and Closings   173
*The Opening Shot — The Closing Shot — Cutting Scenes
Together*

CHAPTER 10: Playing the Visual Environment   183

Giving a Visual Performance — Season and Locale

CHAPTER 11: Basic Camera Staging   191

*Standing — Upstaging — Sitting — Kneeling — Walking —
Crossing in Front of Another Actor — Head Movement —
Eyes — Smiling — Gesturing — Working with the Set*

CHAPTER 12: Script Terminology   213

*The Hard Sell and the Soft Sell — Terms Every Screen Actor
Must Know — The Storyboard*

CHAPTER 13: How Commercials Are Shot   223

*Sequential Order of Shooting — Character Progression —
The "Shooting" Script — Your Relationship with the Crew —
The Actual Shoot — "Roll Camera" — The Shots*

CHAPTER 14: That's a Wrap   239

About the Author   243

Introduction

Perhaps television commercials have given you a little more information than you care to know about the digestive tract, designer jeans, dirty collars, youthful skin, light beer, and lost traveler's checks. I'm with you. After viewing a series of television commercials, I sometimes suffer headaches, nausea, and skin rashes from the overdose. But were it not for Avon calling and Revlon answering, our free television and radio media could not exist.

And frankly, no matter how much we complain about television commercials, plenty of us do respond to them. Why else would a company pay millions of dollars for one minute of network air time during a prime viewing period? With the high cost of a single airing of a commercial, you know each company is going to spend a lot of money on developing one that sells when you see it on network television.

Since you are reading this book, I am going to assume that you are ready to stop just toying with the idea of being in a commercial yourself and get serious about it. You're ahead of all those people who only *think* about getting into this business. Keep in mind that some have to stay on the ground to hold the ladder of success for the few who climb it.

This book is only the beginning. You can't learn to act by reading, any more than you can learn to ski by reading. Reading can give you a good understanding of the process of acting or skiing, but when you get in front of the camera or on the slopes, you'll find it is different from what you originally thought, and perhaps much more difficult. It's a tough business, so you have to have tenacity in order to survive in it. If Columbus had turned back, no one would have blamed him. No one would have remembered him either.

Along with reading this book, you should be attending good commercial acting classes. Take from as many different instructors as possible. A self-taught man usually has a poor teacher and a worse student. But be careful from whom you take classes. Do your homework before you begin with any instructor. In this business there are many actors (the term used here to designate both genders) who go to a series of acting classes taught by people who resemble deranged postal employees.

What this book will give you is a basic understanding of what commercial acting principles and techniques sell and how to sell them. It's important for you to know the basics. Then, when you start auditioning for commercial acting jobs, you'll know the principles set forth in this book and how to apply them. So you're planning ahead. Keep in mind that it wasn't raining when Noah built the ark. The *application* of these principles is the most important aspect of your reading *Acting in the Million Dollar Minute: The Sequel*. And by the way, you don't need to read the original book. In this sequel I've not only updated everything from the original, but have added many more chapters.

In my third and most recent book, *How to Act and Eat at the Same Time: The Sequel* (Amadeus Press, 2004), I discussed the do's and don'ts of auditioning for feature films, television shows, and commercials—the things directors like and dislike about actors during the audition process, what questions to ask and not to ask, what to wear and what not to wear, how not to get nervous, how to obtain an agent, good and bad photographs, a good résumé, contracts, attitudes (good and bad), directors' pet peeves regarding actors during auditions, how to conduct yourself in an audition, callbacks, the audition psychology of landing a role, and so on and so forth.

How to Act and Eat at the Same Time: The Sequel covers the *business* side of acting. I list all the things we like and dislike about actors *personally*, based on very specific research. I record every comment made about every actor I see in auditions. If I saw two hundred actors in one day and there were eight people in the room making comments, and if each person only made one comment (I wish), that would be sixteen hundred comments in that one day alone.

Every night I log all of those comments into a computer. Every six months I go back and pull out of the computer the things we like and dislike about actors. Over the many years that I have been doing this, the data hasn't changed very much. It is extremely consistent from year to year.

In this book, I will use that same collected data to write about the things we like and dislike about commercial actors' *performances*. So please refer to *How to Act and Eat at the Same Time: The Sequel* for the business of show business and the psychology of auditioning, especially as it relates to TV commercial auditions.

The few books out there that deal with commercial acting are usually split into two parts—the business of show business, and how to act in commercials. Since *How to Act and Eat at the Same Time: The Sequel* dealt fully with the former, this book will deal only with the latter. There are a few crossovers from the business side of acting to the performance side. If there is any material in this book that is duplicated in the other, it is only because it was absolutely necessary to include it here.

I will define the lingo and explain the techniques of shooting, describe staging techniques, provide tips on how to position yourself while on camera, discuss the principles for dealing with dialogue and some general acting principles, and then concentrate on dialogue and staging with the product specifically.

This book, unlike others, doesn't have any appendices containing interviews with a few industry professionals. Many times these interviews so contradict each other that I don't know how one makes any sense out of them. That's why I use this extensive research method to paint a concise, clear picture of what we "on the other side of the table" are looking for in your commercial performance.

Also, this book doesn't have pages of "filler" at the end. There are no sections on yoga, exercising, meditation, and so forth. If that's what you're into, there are plenty of excellent acting books out there that you can consult on those subjects.

I have given acting seminars in forty-five states and six countries, spending more time in hotel rooms than a Gideon Bible. Additionally, I have directed many television shows, feature films, and over three hundred national and international commercials. Before becoming a full-time director, I was a professional working actor in all of these media, including hundreds of national commercials. From these experiences, I have accumulated a wealth of information about acting problems that affect everyone from the beginning actor to the seasoned professional. Interestingly, it really doesn't matter what part of the country you're from, or even what country, for that matter; the problems remain consistent.

All of this discussion brings us to you—the commercial actor. *You* are the center of this important world of advertising. *You* will sell the product or service. Companies depend on *you,* the actor, to get their messages across to the public. It could be *your* credibility alone that determines the success or failure of the company sponsoring the commercial! The importance of *you,* the actor, to *me,* the director, is the reason I have written this book.

Learning about show business can be compared to the first time you learned that there was no Santa Claus and later realized it's only one of the many lies you'll be told. Not here, because this book will give it to you straight. The only place where success comes before work is in the dictionary. The road to success is marked with many tempting parking places, but many very ordinary people work in commercials, and so can you. Dreams are like crying babies in a church—they need to be carried out.

Acting in the
Million Dollar Minute

The Importance of Commercials

*It certainly pays to advertise—there are twenty-six mountains
in Colorado that are higher than Pike's Peak.*

*W*hen I'm speaking at a university or acting school out in the hinterlands, the question I'm asked most often is something to the effect of, "Tom, I realize that it's gonna take me a few months or so to get my own television series, so I wanted to know if it would be bad for my career to do some acting in commercials part-time."

That question is so full of misconceptions, I never know where to begin. It's usually asked by some bonehead who has the wisdom of youth and the energy of old age—somebody who'd request a price check at the dollar store. With this type of person I don't engage in a battle of wits; it's unfair to attack anyone who is unarmed.

First of all, commercials are not necessarily the beginning point for actors. Commercial acting jobs can be just as hard to obtain as television and feature film roles—or even much harder. Secondly, acting in commercials is not a part-time or sideline job, at least in the major markets. If you want to work professionally in commercials in those markets, it's a full-time job—training, setting up meetings, always being available for auditions, and so on. It's hard work. You don't work in commercials in the major markets by treating the business as a part-time endeavor. Rip van Winkle is the only man who ever became famous while he slept.

True, we usually see many more people for a commercial audition than for a television or feature film audition, but that's a double-edged sword. If you've been in the business for a long time and have legitimate acting credits, then commercial acting jobs can actually be tougher to get, since we audition so many more people. In other words, the working television or feature film actor is used to competing for jobs against far fewer actors than he would for a commercial.

However, the reverse is true for the beginning actor. Since we audition many more people, a beginning actor might have a better chance of getting into a commercial audition versus the other visual media. It stands to reason that, since we see more people, the odds of a newcomer's obtaining a commercial audition are greater. But since we see more people, there's more competition. See the conflict here?

The Commercial "Type"

Many times I hear agents and acting instructors say such things as, "You're so commercial looking," "You're such a good type for commercials," "The commercial market will love you," and so on. What really is a commercial "type"?

In the early days of commercials, good-looking people did tend to work much more than your average Joe. The idea back then was that commercials should be bigger than real life, and pretty people would sell more products. Luckily for most actors, this idea doesn't hold water in today's world. Advertisers have since found that for most products other than beauty-related ones, the public identifies more with real, facially challenged people than with models.

All physical types work in commercials. Perhaps you're so large that Richard Simmons won't deal you a meal and your photo has to be taken from a satellite. Maybe your body has more nooks and crannies than an English muffin and you have more chins than Chinatown. Or maybe you're so skinny you could do push-ups under the door.

Perhaps your hair was styled with a Weed Wacker. Maybe you're so old that you drove chariots to high school and knew Alexander the Great when he was only mediocre. There's work for you in commercials no matter what physical type you are or what age you happen to be.

Having said all this, there are a few physical restrictions that can apply to certain products. If you're so large you can't make it through the arches at McDonalds or can do the wave by yourself, you'll have a harder time being cast in a fast-food commercial. Advertisers might worry that people would think of their product as the reason you have more rolls than a bread shop. But other products could be open season for such an actor.

It is perhaps true that if you're missing so many teeth it appears as though your tongue is in jail and nicer heads have been seen on a witch doctor's belt, you might have a harder time being cast in a toothpaste commercial than someone who has a perfect set of teeth and a pleasant face. If your teeth are so yellow that cars slow down when they see you smile, toothpaste commercials might not be your thing. But even then, maybe you could be the "before." So never discount your looks as necessarily a deterrent to obtaining commercial acting jobs.

People will say to me something to the effect of, "But, Tom, with my looks I give Freddy Krueger nightmares. Is that going to hurt me?" It all depends on what we're looking for. If we're looking for someone who could play the title role in *Alien,* your appearance wouldn't hurt you—it would actually help you. If we're looking for the perfect face, then it could hurt you. Your looks will help you or hurt you only to the extent that they do or don't meet what we happen to be looking for at the moment you walk in the door.

Show Me the Money

The pay is so exceptional for acting in commercials that many stars are begging to do them. Every year more money is made by actors in commercials than by actors in all stage plays combined. Believe it or not, more money is made by actors in commercials than in all feature films combined, including ones shown in the theaters combined with all video and DVD sales nationally and internationally.

It's pretty easy to see why. Commercials employ more actors than do television shows and feature films. In a union commercial or television show that is not a buy-out (where you're paid a one-time fee for all airings), actors are paid every time their commercial airs. A majority of television shows air only a few times in their entire life span. However, a commercial may air many times a day, for many years. So an actor may work only one day in a commercial but still be paid for many, many days of work, days on which he didn't actually do anything. Do the math.

The question I mentioned at the beginning of the chapter, about whether it would be detrimental to do some commercial acting jobs, just shows how naive many actors are about the world of acting in commercials. If you gave these actors a penny for their thoughts, you'd have change coming back. Let's be honest here: some of the finest actors in show business are found in commercials.

In fact, the hardest acting job you'll ever have just might be in a commercial. You have to create a very likable character, say dialogue that you wouldn't normally say and that isn't very conversational (how many times in real life do you see a woman running down the beach talking about how terrific her feminine deodorant is?), and make that dialogue come out to exactly fifteen, thirty, or sixty seconds, all while appearing natural. Make no mistake—commercials tell a story, just as television shows and feature films do. They just have to do it much more quickly and precisely.

The misconception is that actors in commercials aren't actually acting at all. That's because they're so good at it! The better the actor is at his craft, the more you believe he isn't acting at all. Very gifted actors have the ability to make you think they are just normal, every-day people you'd meet on the street. The last thing a director wants is for someone from the public to view his commercial and then say, "Wow, what a great acting job." If it looks like acting, the commercial is dead on arrival. The exception would be a well-known celebrity or star who is endorsing a product. But even then, the commercial will die if that well-known person seems to be acting, rather than behaving naturally.

How many times have you watched a commercial and said to yourself something like, "Where'd they get that pinhead? I could do that." You're thinking this guy couldn't spell AT&T and that Leonard Nimoy wants to go in search of his brain. Many times we *want* you to think that we just grabbed this guy off the street, that he's missing a few brain cells and could flunk a urine test. The reality is that almost all of the actors you see in national commercials are very well trained and accomplished in their trade.

I've had the good fortune in my life to have the incredible pleasure of working with one of the finest actors in this business. Remember the toilet paper commercials where Mr. Whipple says, "Please, don't squeeze the Charmin"? That actor is Dick Wilson. He is in the *Guinness Book of World Records* as the most successful commercial actor of all time. (Interestingly, the first commercial he filmed for Charmin was shot in Flushing, New York. That's a fact!)

What you might not know is that Dick's career includes regular roles in many television series and even starring roles in feature films. Before Charmin he had a major career under way, but few people in the public knew who he was until he landed the Charmin campaign. (He jokingly says that when he started doing Charmin commercials his career "landed in the toilet.")

He is so good at what he does that anytime we're out to dinner people will come up to him and converse about Charmin as though he worked for the toilet paper company. People actually think his regular job was to keep people from squeezing the Charmin. Successful commercial actors make their jobs look easy. But the reality is that it's hard work, as you're going to realize by the time you finish this book. Opportunity typically favors those who have paid the price of years of preparation.

Yes, there are exceptions to this rule. There are some actors who have very little talent and become big stars. But that's just what they are—exceptions. It makes you wonder what deals Britney Spears and Paris Hilton made with the devil.

Commercials Are Big Business

Most people think of television as shows interrupted by a bunch of commercials. We in the entertainment business, however, think of television as commercials interrupted by a bunch of television shows. That's because commercials pay our salaries and the cost of producing the television shows you watch. Without commercials, you'd have to pay a fee to view television shows.

We in the industry take commercials very seriously. The average national commercial costs $300,000 to $1 million or more to produce. And that's just for the few days' work of filming it. Before it was shot, bundles of bills were spent for all of the pre-production costs. And after it's shot, more money is spent in post-production—editing, screenings, special effects, and so on. Then many more millions are spent airing those commercials. In 2004, for example, thirty seconds of commercial air time during the SuperBowl cost over $1.5 million. We're talking about *one airing!*

Want to know some statistics? Ninety-nine percent of the households in the United States have a television set. Sixty-six percent have three or more. There's a television playing in the average U.S. household for about seven hours a day. The average human being spends about four hours a day watching television. The average U.S. resident will spend over one year of his life watching television commercials.

An advertiser can reach more people in one commercial than in all print advertising combined. And he can air it over and over again for maximum effect.

The Importance of Commercials for the Actor

The importance of commercials to a company is evident. Many people, however, don't realize the importance of commercials to an actor. I can't tell you how many times directors have seen an actor in a commercial and then tracked him down to cast him in a television show or feature film. Many well-known actors are starring in feature films and television shows today because someone first spotted them in a commercial. The exposure of one television commercial far outpaces the exposure in any other format, owing primarily to the frequency with which it is aired.

Actors who have heads so big they could show up on radar think this type of acting is beneath them. I guess this starts with the "artsy-fartsy" type of stage actors who think that any type of acting other than that done on the stage is beneath them. Some of them believe that acting in a commercial would be selling out, and they would just as soon spontaneously combust. Where this notion began I can't imagine. Not only can a commercial acting job begin a career and even restart a star's fading career, but it can also free up an actor's time so that he can be available to go on auditions for "real" acting jobs.

So many actors have to support themselves by taking other jobs while they try to get auditions. Many actors haven't actually worked in this business since Burger King was a prince. Some have been on welfare so long that their faces appear on food stamps. So it's much better to be saying "Can I get you some fries with that?" in a commercial airing on television than to be saying it live down at your local fast-food joint. If television and feature film roles are your ultimate goal, having a commercial on the air can support you while you work on your "real" career full time.

Do I Have to Move to Los Angeles or New York?

The short answer is no. Commercials are cast and shot all over the world. But it's true that most national commercials are cast in the two major markets of Los Angeles and New York. In fact, about 90 percent of the national commercials now airing were cast in or near those markets. And, frankly, for the amount of money we spend on a national commercial, an airline ticket is a drop in the bucket to us. So we don't mind flying actors from those two major markets to anywhere in the world in order to shoot a commercial. When you look at the statistics, it becomes obvious that Los Angeles or New York is the place to be if you want to be in a position to audition for the majority of national commercials.

On the other hand, many local and some regional commercials are cast in markets all over the world, in some of the smallest cities. Perhaps you live in a town so small your school taught driver's education and sex education in the same car. Local commercials are shot in such towns. Just turn on the tube in whatever city in which you happen to reside, and you'll see many local commercials airing.

You can get good experience from acting in these local commercials. This experience will be invaluable to you if you eventually decide to move to Los Angeles or New York. You can learn the ropes and work on your craft. And by acting in these local commercials you can gain confidence—one of the most important things you can have in an audition.

You should move to the major markets only when you feel as though you have exhausted the work in your local area. When you feel you can't grow any more as an actor in your local town, then it might be time to make the plunge, if this is your ultimate goal.

But beware! I can't tell you how many actors I meet every day who, having become extremely successful in their local markets, move to Los Angeles or New York, become frustrated, and then make like E.T. and go home.

Of course, one advantage to moving to a major market is that you will be able to tell everyone you were once an "L.A. actor" or a "New York actor." For some reason, once an actor has become an "L.A. actor" or a "New York actor" and then moved back to his hometown, everyone thinks more highly of him. Many of these actors have a chip on their shoulders, which indicates there is wood a little higher up.

This theory also works in the directing field. I was an "L.A. director" for many years. Then I was hired to be a director for feature films at Universal Studios in Orlando, Florida. After directing five feature films there, I was called into a meeting with a new studio head, where I was told that one of the films I very much wanted to direct was "a really big feature and needed an L.A. director." I had lost my Los Angeles status! The guy who told me that wasn't very high up on the intelligence chain and is still watching *The Never-Ending Story*. Since I have been back working in Los Angeles for many years now, I have my "L.A. director" status back.

If you move to either of these Twin Cities—Sodom or Gomorrah—bring lots of dough. This isn't a book about how to live in New York or Los Angeles, but suffice it to say that most of the housing in those cities needs refurbishment—it could use a good coat of fire. Some of the neighborhoods are so bad, anyone not missing a body part is considered a sissy. Many of the supermarkets have pictures of missing cops on the backs of milk cartons.

In L.A., you'll definitely need a car. Los Angeles is basically ninety-seven suburbs in search of a city. Drive so that your driver's license will expire before you do. Be careful on the freeways; everyone drives a tad rapidly. Keep in mind that it's better to step on the brake and be laughed at than to push the gas and be cried over. A car is like good manners—useless in New York, essential everywhere else.

The Birthing Process of a Commercial

How a commercial goes from the concept to the actual airing is a long process. I will attempt to explain it as simply as possible here, but keep in mind that for the sake of simplicity, I've left out a number of steps.

First, executives from a particular company decide that they need to advertise. Maybe they're selling a new product line, or perhaps they just want to boost sales on an existing one. They first decide who their audience is—age group, sex, education level, and so on. They do lots, and I mean *lots,* of research to find out who specifically is interested in their product(s).

These executives hire an ad agency to begin the process of formulating a commercial concept. At the ad agency, account executives come up with ideas for a campaign. Once a specific idea has been decided upon, a copywriter comes up with various scripts supporting that idea. Then these ideas are pitched to the account executive(s). The presentation can include, among other things, drawings, storyboards, and slides.

After much discussion, debate, and compromise, everyone eventually approves a specific script, either because they have been outranked or because they have to go along with whatever the majority agrees upon. Then come many more debates and discussions on how to rework the script to "everyone's satisfaction," although that is probably an oxymoron.

Usually no one is really happy with the final script since there was so much compromise involved. The script conference is where everybody talks, nobody listens, and afterward everyone disagrees. I've learned that you don't really finish a script—at some point you just abandon it.

Production companies that might shoot the commercial are then contacted. These production companies present their budgets, schedules, ideas, and so forth. After many more discussions and debates, arguments, and hissy fits, one of these companies wins the campaign. Then more discussions, debates, and general bickering take place between the account executives from the ad agency and the people from the production company—producer, director, art director(s), and others. These guys never grab on to a good chance to shut up.

Next, a casting director is selected. This casting director has many meetings and discussions with the account executive(s) and the director. These discussions include what physical types are needed for this particular ad. Many times the casting director ends up not knowing what to look for in actors since the director and account executives don't see the characters in the same way. In fact, my experience has been that even the account executives don't agree among themselves. The confused casting director then contacts agents and informs them what types she *thinks* are needed. The agents then submit photos of their clients who might possibly be right for the parts.

The casting director weeds through all the photos and, depending on the relationship between the casting director and director, will decide—either individually or jointly, if they even have any input at all with the director—who should be auditioned for this commercial. The casting director then phones the agents to inform them who will be seen on the audition. In turn, the agents then inform the actors that they are going to audition for so-and-so product at such-and-such a time on this-or-that date.

These actors are auditioned. Many discussions between the members of the "committee" (director, account executives, representatives from the product, etc.) take place as they review the tapes from the auditions. The committee is made up of the unable, appointed by the unwilling, to do the unnecessary. These committees delegate all the authority, shift all the blame, and take all the credit. Basically, they are a great way to waste time. I've participated in many of these meetings over the years and have come to the conclusion that to get something done, a committee should consist of only three people, two of whom should be absent.

I can tell you from experience that arguing with these guys is like trying to read a newspaper in a high wind. I've learned to never argue with a fool—people might not notice the difference. Also, I don't argue with idiots—they'll drag you down to their level and then beat you with experience.

It's a tough and diverse group. Some of the people in the committee look as if they know where Jimmy Hoffa was buried. Some are highly educated, and others quit high school because there was an opening on the lube rack. Finally, after many debates, which sometimes become extremely petty, the committee compiles a list of actors for the callbacks.

As the committee members drink a mix of Perrier and club soda, they end up seeing each other's lists, so the callbacks can involve many actors. After the actors are reauditioned, the committee meets again to debate, bicker, and bitch about who should be used in this spot. At some point, we'll all more or less agree on the actors who are right for the various roles. The actor(s) chosen might in fact have been no one's first choice. Usually, the director has more power in casting than anyone else, with the exception of the client. Fortunately, the client usually tries to accommodate the director, since the director is responsible for the acting and production quality of the commercial.

After the cast has been assembled, a number of details have to be worked out, over the smallest of which, again, many more debates take place. A few days or weeks later, the committee, the actors, and the crew meet for the shooting, which can take anywhere from a day up to a week. While the shooting is taking place, the director has to again debate, discuss, and compromise with the committee, of which he is a member.

Many times these discussions take place right in front of the actors in between takes. I've had committee members asking me why I wanted the actor I was directing—right in front of that actor! It's downright embarrassing—kind of like sitting with your parents and watching a movie that shows full-frontal nudity.

After everyone's headaches, caused by the bickering from the shoot day, are gone, the committee (which by this point sometimes has members who won't speak to each other) meets in the editing room. The editing room is a real audio-visual delight: even more discussions and debates take place, producing even more headaches and possible suicides, before the editing of the commercial is finished. Directors try to keep cool heads in the editing room. I personally try to act in such a way that when death comes, my mourners will outnumber the cheering section.

Then, if it's a national ad, it is usually test-marketed, meaning that it's shown in special theaters nationwide to groups of people who will fill out a survey. This survey hopefully will indicate how much the audience liked or disliked the ad. Then the Klingon committee meets to discuss and debate the results.

More bitching takes place about the meaning of the results, since no one really agrees on what the results indicate. It's the old glass-half-full/glass-half-empty debate. As you probably know, statistics lie. Each committee member makes the results match his preconceived notions. That's so each member can say "I told you so" without actually appearing to say that. Think of the director as a navigator on the Sea of Confusion. In the end, the overwhelming conclusion is that no conclusion can be drawn.

However, at some point everyone is so frustrated that they just agree to disagree. More research and perhaps even more test-marketing are done—and more headaches triggered—before the commercial ends up on television.

After all that, you're probably wondering how some of the ads you see ever end up on the air. Not to worry—we wonder, too. It's so unbelievable that a commercial ever gets finished and ends up on the air that I've considered calling Ripley's.

Crawling Around on the Floor Acting like a Lion

This book is about *acting* in commercials. We're not going to discuss how to "crawl around on the floor and act like a lion." I'm not putting that type of class down, it's just that this isn't that type of book. The truth is, I'm a simple guy and I just don't get all that stuff.

When I was an actor, way back when "swingers" were people who relaxed on the front porch, I just didn't understand much of the psychobabble many acting teachers used. This is not a put-down of those classes or teachers, not by any stretch of the imagination. They are on a totally different plane than I am, perhaps a much higher one. I guess they know their fields, but this simple mind of mine never comprehended what they were talking about. Many acting instructors just seem to make acting so much more complicated than it really has to be.

Consequently, I know this book will be understood by all. Even if you're the type that tries to read an audio book and your train of thought stops at every station, you'll have no problem understanding the concepts set out here. Regardless of what many people in this industry might tell you, acting in commercials is not rocket science. I didn't say it was easy. I'm not implying that it doesn't take a lot of work and dedication. I'm only saying that so many acting books and drama classes make the whole commercial acting process complicated. You'll find, as you go through this book, that this isn't the case here.

We directors really respect what you do. You will make us look good or bad. The success or failure of an entire company can depend on your performance. I, as the director, will be judged by how well or poorly you do in any commercial I direct. You represent the company and, frankly, me.

Contrary to what most actors believe, we like actors. Yes, casting is the last thing we do when it comes to putting together a commercial campaign. Sometimes we make final casting decisions the day before the commercial is to be shot. Many actors take this to mean that we put a low priority on the actors and the casting process. Nothing could be further from the truth.

In fact, the argument could be made that we save the best for last. As you can now see, there are so many details to be worked out before the actual shooting of a commercial that perhaps we want to get all of the particulars out of the way first. Then and only then can we devote all of our attention to the casting process.

When Does the Audition Begin?

An audition begins when you first hear about it, and the actual shoot really begins when you're booked to shoot the commercial. Those are the times when you start thinking about how you're going to perform.

In the case of an audition, you start performing immediately after your agent informs you that you have been selected to audition. You begin thinking about wardrobe, character, the locale of the audition, the money, and so on.

When you're on your way to an audition, you are constantly thinking about how you're going to perform. Start being nice to everyone at or around the audition. When you arrive in the parking lot, that person you cut off to get into that one particular parking space just might be the director. The person you complain to in the restroom about the audition just might be the client. More than a few actors have lost acting jobs because they were rude to someone before they arrived in the actual audition room. The squeaky wheel doesn't always get the grease—sometimes it gets replaced.

Furthermore, there are directors who sit in the lobby and just watch "who's naughty and who's nice" while the actors are waiting to audition. Of course, you should be nice to everyone all the time, but if you're not generally a very nice person, try to temper your negativity when you're auditioning.

Be especially nice to secretaries and assistants. These are the casting directors of tomorrow. And they report to the casting director and director. I can't tell you how many times I'll get a tip from a secretary or an assistant about an actor who obviously went to the Martha Stewart charm school. Some actors are the type that could go to Friendly's and get punched in the face. How you treat your fellow actors in the lobby is a reflection of how you're going to treat your fellow actors and crew members in an actual shoot.

Other actors in an audition might try to make themselves seem more important than you. They'll talk about all the acting jobs they have been turning down. Please don't believe the trash you hear in the lobby. No one can make you feel inferior without your consent. People who try to whittle you down are only trying to reduce you to their size. If criticism could cause someone to quit, the skunk would be extinct. Don't play their game. Don't brag, either—it's not the whistle that pulls the train. Always keep your words soft and sweet, in case you have to eat them.

Once you walk into the audition room, the actual "performance" *on camera* begins with the slate, which is the subject of the next chapter.

The Slate

You never get a second chance to make a first impression.

*T*he slate is the stating of your name at the beginning of your audition, whether you're auditioning for a television show, feature film, or commercial. In a commercial audition we see literally hundreds of actors day after day for each role. We have to have some way of identifying each actor. Many times I'll have twenty or more pages full of actor's names for a single day of auditioning. And we may be auditioning for many weeks!

Most actors slough off the slate, thinking it's nothing more than a way of transmitting their name to us. Very few actors actually treat the slate as part of their audition. This is one of the single biggest mistakes actors make in commercial auditions, or any audition, for that matter.

The Importance of the Slate

The slate is the most important part of any commercial audition. The fact is, in most auditions we don't watch the entire playback of most actors' performances. If we see two hundred people in one day, we're not going to watch all two hundred playbacks in their entirety that evening. In fact, if we watch ten full playbacks, that would be considered a really good day. Five is probably more like it.

What just about every director does is fast-forward from slate to slate to slate without ever actually watching the commercials. "Unfair!" you respond. If you have read *How to Act and Eat at the Same Time: The Sequel,* you'll remember that this isn't a fair business—never has been, never will be. If you're looking for fair, then you need to look for another business. However, you'll be disappointed there too, because in reality no business is fair.

We hear the "this isn't fair" argument day after day. Face it, life ain't fair. Ginger Rogers did everything Fred Astaire did, backward and in high heels. Who got top billing? How come the most lucrative endorsement deals go to the best-performing male athletes and the best-looking female ones? Why do sixty-year-old male actors get to play action heroes while female actors of the same age get to play their mothers? Let me repeat: life ain't fair!

Let's use a dating comparison. When you go on a blind date, once you open the door, just how long does it take you to decide whether this is going to be a good date or a bad date? If you say over three minutes, you're lonely. Men, if, when you open the door, you realize she's been boarded more times than Amtrak, you *immediately* decide whether this is good or bad. Women, if, when you open the door, you realize listening to him makes you think of a river—small at the head and big at the mouth—you *immediately* decide this isn't going to be a fun evening. Maybe you wanted someone a little closer to the top of the food chain.

We're talking about a four-hour date here, and most people are going to make a snap decision about its success or lack thereof in a few seconds. This is *really* unfair, isn't it? In fact, you're giving the blind date less time to impress you, proportionally, than we give your slate!

Think back to when you were in grade school. Didn't you sum up just how hard or easy the entire year was going to be with a particular teacher on the basis of the first day? Just after I graduated from college, I substitute-taught for a very short time. I learned a big lesson:

the students sum up a substitute teacher in a matter of seconds. In no time flat, they figure out what they can and can't get away with. Remember the game "Sink the Sub"?

When I would first take over a class for a few days, I would quickly find one student who was doing something wrong that was so minute, normally no one would care. I'd send that one student out of the room to stand in the hallway for five minutes; then I'd let him back in. This got the students' attention. Then I could lighten up on them for the next few days. Funny thing—I usually had no problems for the rest of my short teaching stint with any particular class.

Your slate makes that same first and lasting impression. The difference is, I had many hours for the students' opinions to eventually change after I gave them that first dramatic introduction to myself. But you don't have hours. You don't even have minutes. You have literally less than one minute, usually less than half a minute, after your slate to make a favorable or not-so-favorable impression. The slate gives us more information about you than you can imagine.

Hitting Your Mark

When you enter the audition room, someone will tell you to "hit your mark." Some actors I've said this to have actually asked, "Hit what?" When an actor doesn't know how to hit a mark, we immediately realize that he has never acted in a commercial and that he won't be phoning Mensa. In fact, he's obviously never been to a commercial audition, and, for that matter, he's probably never even taken a legitimate, competent commercial acting class.

There will be a mark on the floor in the actual audition room. You are expected to hit that mark with precision. We've set up the lights in such a way as to be the most favorable to you if you're on that mark. We've set the camera up just the way that frames you best if you are where you're supposed to be. We've even focused the camera to that mark.

So if you're "off the mark," you're probably in less than favorable lighting, on the edge or completely out of the frame, and probably out of focus. If those things don't bother you, then go ahead and do what most actors do—just get somewhere near the mark. Many actors come from stage acting and are used to kind of being in a general area of the stage at not necessarily an exact point in the script. However, we're no longer on a stage here. So these actors need to get with the program.

If you watch a few of the late-night talk shows, you might notice the host's mark. Usually, at the beginning of the show, the host comes out from behind a curtain and walks right to a mark before he begins his monologue. It's not a coincidence that when the host stops, he is exactly centered in the frame, his face is well lit, and he is in perfect focus.

There are basically two types of marks—an "X" and a "T." If there's an "X," you should position your body directly over the "X." That doesn't mean that you are over the "X" while leaning on one leg. When I say "over the 'X,'" I mean "over the 'X.'" One foot should be on one side of the "X" and the other foot on the other side of it. It's important that your body be aligned so that your head is also right over the center of that "X." No leaning! Leaning not only puts you out of focus, possibly on the edge of the frame or completely out of it, and possibly in less than favorable lighting, but it also makes you look crooked in that frame. In fact, some actors look so crooked the Mafia would be their reform group.

If there's a "T" marked on the floor, then one foot should go on one side of the vertical line and the other foot on the other side of that line, with both feet just behind the horizontal line. Again, this doesn't mean that you place your feet properly and then lean heavily on one leg.

And watch that rocking that many actors do once the camera begins rolling. You could easily be rocking out of frame to the left, back into the frame, and then out of the frame to the right, or vice versa. Sometimes I can hardly see an actor during his audition because he rocked so much that all I see is a flash of a person flying by every once in a while.

When you rock back and forth, we're wondering if perhaps you went on an ocean cruise recently and are still rocking with the waves. Or maybe you got into the liquor cabinet the night before. I figure many of these rocking actors live on a fault line. Rocking not only shows us how little you understand about frame lines, it also makes you appear so uncoordinated that you could trip over a cordless phone.

It's common for actors to be fired simply because they can't hit marks. If you're not able to hit marks, I won't be able to get a particular show or commercial shot, because it'll be so messy it won't end up on the air. As an example, watch a daytime serial (also called a soap opera, because back in the old radio days most of the afternoon serials were sponsored by soap companies). I was an actor on and off *General Hospital* for twelve years in the 1970s and 1980s, and I can tell you that missed marks were one of the directors' biggest complaints.

You can actually see daytime serial actors looking for their marks. Keep in mind that these actors are memorizing, blocking, rehearsing, and shooting a hundred or more pages per day. They are doing the equivalent of a play a day. And they are doing it five days a week, fifty-two weeks a year, with no reruns! They have very little time to rehearse, so they are constantly looking for their marks.

Whenever I teach a weekend seminar, I usually ask someone in the audience to bring a copy of a daytime serial they have on tape. The next day, when I view the show with the actors who are participating in the seminar, I show them how many times the actors on the tape keep looking down as they move. The seminar participants are always amazed. When I see them years later, they almost always remark to me that they haven't been able to watch a daytime serial since. People on sitcoms and in movies of the week, feature films, and commercials are also looking for marks. It's just that actors in those genres have much more rehearsal time, so it isn't really that noticeable.

Actors aren't the only people who have to hit marks during filming. Stunt actors have to hit them when doing stunts. I might, for instance, have five cars crashing in a particular scene. I may need one of the cars to roll three times and another to roll four times, while having both cars end up stopping on marks. After all, if the cars miss their marks, they might be out of focus or completely out of frame. This is one of the main reasons we do stunts over and over again during an actual shoot.

You might have to drive a car to a mark. How many times in television shows, feature films, and commercials have you seen a car pull right into frame and stop? Do you realize how hard it is to do this? The frame size may look big on the screen, but in reality we're talking about stopping a car right on a mark—dead center—to accomplish this difficult task.

If the street isn't seen we can use sandbags. The actor just drives the car into the sandbags—or, more likely, crew members will push the car from behind right into the sandbags—and it will automatically stop on the mark. Furniture, props, the camera dolly, the boom man, and so on all have marks. When you arrive on a set you'll be amazed at how many marks are all over the floor. In fact, if you ever have the opportunity to see a sitcom being shot, take a look at the floor and you'll see marks everywhere. We can use anything for marks during actual shoots. If two actors are walking down a sidewalk, for example, I might place a leaf, a twig, or a rock where the actors are supposed to stop.

Not only do actors have to stop on marks so that they are in frame, in focus, and well lit, but they also have to hit "focus-pull" marks. Let's suppose, for example, that you have to say the line "I really like this hamburger from Burger World" while walking down a hallway. You might have to hit a focus-pull mark on the word "hamburger." That doesn't mean you stop when you say "hamburger." You may have to keep walking as we pull the focus to you on that word and that mark. However, if you're not on that mark when you say that word, you could be totally out of focus.

In this example, we're only talking about hitting one mark on one word. In an actual shoot, though, you might hit focus-pull marks on many words in one sentence. Doing this while staying in character and making it all look and sound natural is much more difficult than it appears.

Getting a scene that works requires that many people and objects end up where they are supposed to be—on marks. The audition process is our first clue as to how well you do or don't hit marks. Hitting or not hitting your mark tells the director a lot about how well you will or won't perform on the shoot day, should you be hired. Smart directors are watching for that during your audition.

The Frame Lines

It's extremely important that you know where the frame lines are during your audition, and during the actual shoot, for that matter. It really doesn't matter where the camera is physically located; that won't really tell you much about where the frame lines are. For instance, the camera could be in the back of the room, while a zoom lens is used to put you into a tight close-up. By the same token, the camera could be fairly close to you, but be using a wide-angle lens that is pulled back, so the shot might not be as close as it seems.

As soon as you hit your mark, you should ask, "Where are the frame lines?" or "How are you framing this?" This impresses directors. We would then know, or at least think, that you are camera savvy. Knowing where the frame lines are will also give you valuable information as to how much movement you can or, more accurately, can't perform during your audition. It also gives you some idea as to how "big" or "small" you might want to play the character visually.

If your image in the frame is small, a large movement of your eyebrows, for example, might not be that big a deal. However, if the camera has a tight shot of your face, full frame, even small eyebrow movements will probably become extreme, and you may look like a Barnum and Bailey clown, making it appear as though your family tree could stand a lot of pruning.

When you ask for the frame lines, the director or casting director isn't really going to show you all four lines of the square that appears on the television screen. What they will usually do is hold one hand out flat to show the bottom of the frame.

Think of television as a perfect square. In reality it isn't, but it's close enough. I realize that wide-screen television is the wave of the future, but right now, in 2005, we're still using the old format for almost all auditions. So if the director holds his hand out flat right at the middle of his neck, at mid-chest, or at his waist, for example, you should be able to fill in the rest of the square.

This is important information because it lets you know exactly how much you can or can't move your head and other parts of your body. There is nothing worse in an audition than a bobbing head that is constantly going in and out of frame, making it appear as though you should register at the Centers for Disease Control.

When I was an actor, way back when "hardware" meant hammers, screwdrivers, and pliers, I remember an acting teacher once telling me to never ask for the frame lines. This teacher's reasoning was that the technical stuff was for the director and other crew members to worry about, and that the actor's only concern should be with his performance. He said you should act with your whole body anyway, so why would this type of technical information be of any use to a "real" actor?

At the time, I thought this teacher was perhaps a genius. I have since learned that the difference between genius and stupidity is that genius has its limits. Not to question his intelligence, but I have since come to the realization that he is neither left-brained or right-brained. Now that I'm a director, I couldn't disagree with him more on this point.

Yes, you should act with your whole body, but it's nice to know what's in frame and what's out—especially if we're talking about your face. For instance, it's nice to know that your hand gestures aren't flying all over the screen in front of your face. By knowing the frame lines, you'll know your physical limitations onscreen. Experienced actors are very aware of how we're framing a scene.

This teacher had obviously never sat on the other side of the camera during an actual audition. We're so pleased when someone asks, and even more pleased when they use the knowledge to stay in frame. Please don't ask us for information about the frame lines and then not use it. If we gave you the frame lines and you then bobbed in and out of frame, it would show us that you don't take direction very well.

On the other hand, when an actor does use this information and follows the frame lines, right off the bat I think this actor is trained and understands one of the director's main concerns when it comes to working with actors on camera. You're letting the director know that you understand the camera. That's refreshing to us, because many actors who have just come from the stage don't.

One good way to see how the frame lines affect your performance size is to use your home video camera. First, set the camera up for a long shot (one in which the whole body is shown). Stand in front of the camera and say a few lines of dialogue. Next, set the camera for a medium shot (from the waist up) and say those same few lines of dialogue with the same intensity, volume, and energy. Then set the camera for a close-up (face only) and perform those lines in exactly the same way. Finally, set the camera for an extreme close-up (from the eyes to the mouth) only, using the same performance level. (See chapter 13 for more information on these types of shots.)

Notice how different the same dialogue with the same intensity looks on camera with the different framings. Notice that the farther away the camera is, with no zoom (wider frame), the smaller the action comes across on camera. Conversely, notice that when the camera is closer (physically or because a zoom lens is being used), the larger and more energetic the same action becomes.

It is extremely important that you practice this exercise in front of a camera. I have found that actors who really know this business work very well with the frame lines. When I'm directing stars in motion pictures, some of them will ask not only what the frame lines are, but also what lens I am using. These are true pros who thoroughly understand the filming process. I've also noticed that generally, the more an actor knows about what we're doing, the better his performance comes across on camera.

Your performance level will be determined by the framing, so why wouldn't you want to have this key information when you're auditioning? To that teacher who said the information isn't useful, I say, "Go sit in an audition and then watch the playbacks." He would come away with a totally different attitude about the frame question. Frankly, if stupidity were a crime, he'd get the electric chair.

What We Look For in the Slate

According to the data extracted from my computer, there are essentially two things we look for in the slate. First, we almost always want warmth in a commercial slate, and usually in the entire commercial audition, for that matter. I guess there are a few extreme exceptions where warmth wouldn't be right for a certain character, but that's just what they would be—extreme exceptions. And remember, you're not performing the actual commercial yet, you're just doing your slate.

This is a commercial, for goodness' sake. Some people are so mean-looking in their slate! Yes, we want that family look, but not as in Manson. I can't tell you how many times a particular client has fast-forwarded after an actor's slate while saying something like, "America will never love that grouch."

Commercials almost always give upbeat, positive messages, and we don't want to use actors who are such downers that a chain of self-image schools could use them as bad examples. Even casket commercials, for example, are positive. So make sure you project warmth in your slate. It is our first introduction to how warm you are or aren't going to be during your audition and, ultimately, your performance in a given commercial.

There are two great ways to warm up a slate. First of all, you could smile. Wow, what a revelation! You're now thinking that I have a keen sense for the obvious. I do; but unfortunately, most actors don't. You'd be surprised how many actors on commercial auditions can't muster up a smile even for their slate. Our feeling is that if you can't get a smile going during a few-seconds-long slate, how are you going to keep up a genuine smile during an entire commercial shoot when we're doing take after take? When the slate is cold, it gives us more incentive to fast-forward to the next slate even before we watch *any* of your performance.

I'm sure you've heard many times that it actually takes more muscles to frown than to smile. This is a physiological fact. Smiling is actually good for you. You probably know people who walk around frowning all the time, making it appear as though their lifelong ambition is to own a fireworks stand. Don't be one of them. Or, at least, don't be one of them when you're in a commercial audition. Smiles and frowns cost nothing, but the difference in effect is enormous. Your smile is the most important thing you'll wear on an audition.

It is best to say, "Hi, good morning. My name is . . . ," or, "Hi, good afternoon. My name is . . . ." There are casting directors who will tell you not to do this because you might have auditioned in the morning and the director might be watching playbacks in the evening, or vice versa. Nonsense! We realize the auditions we're watching were taped and aren't live. Give us some credit!

The important reason for adding these few extra words to your slate, besides warming it up, is that they extend your slate by a few seconds, so your slate is actually slightly longer than most of the other actors'. Most actors only say their name, or just say "Hi" and then their name. The extra time it takes to say these few extra words actually messes up our rhythm as we fast-forward from slate to slate to slate. And whenever our fast-forwarding rhythm is messed up, we tend to watch that actor's commercial. We're kind of in a hypnotic state after seeing a hundred or so commercial playbacks, so shaking things up a little doesn't hurt your chances.

Now, don't take this to an extreme. If we're doing a McDonald's commercial, for example, some actors will start off talking about how much they love Big Macs. That's great. However, nobody cares. The slate should not be any longer than what I've just said, unless we ask you to slate your agency and/or other information.

The other end of the extreme is when actors say just their name, and usually very coldly: "Kitty Litter." Or, perhaps even worse, they state their name and then immediately begin delivering their commercial. It is so straightforward and matter-of-fact that we get no sense whatsoever of any warmth from that actor.

Believe it or not, a majority of actors do this kind of slate. We're thinking they should consider a career as a crash dummy. In fact, it's almost an arrogant way of presenting yourself. It's as though you're telling us you don't need to show any personality because we should just know you by name only. Trust me: we don't.

We may or may not ask you to also slate your agency. If we ask for it, don't slate this way: "Kitty Litter, Dewey, Cheatum, and Howe Agency." Again, this comes off as too cold and gives us no extra information about you. Put in the "Hi, good morning, my name is...," or the "Hi, good afternoon, my name is...," instead of just listing your name and agency.

The second thing we look for in the slate is, do we understand what you're saying? It's extremely important that we understand you when you present your name. Not understanding your name is like winking at an attractive person in the dark: you know what you're doing, but no one else does. On the highway of life, you're a stalled vehicle.

For every ten actors I want to call back, there are at least three I can't because they rushed their name and so I don't know who they are. How many times have you come home, turned on your answering machine, and heard something like, "Hi, this is $*@&* and my number is %$^%86"? Sound familiar?

Suppose you go house hunting. After visiting about twenty homes you'll be confusing the living room of one house with the bedroom of another. In fact, at some point there'll be homes you can't even remember visiting. The same thing happens in commercial auditions. We have many pages of actors' names listed in alphabetical order. When you run your first and last names together, it becomes very unclear where to start looking for your name on those pages.

Once I was directing a national commercial in New York City. We were looking at tapes of actors who had auditioned in Los Angeles. The commercial was to be shot in New York within two days, so we had no time to waste. One actor came on the tape who was physically perfect for the part. We needed a strange-looking character, out of the mainstream, very elderly, overweight, with unusual facial features.

When this particular actor appeared on the tape, I knew we had our guy. He had the perfect huge ears—I wondered why he didn't get the tusks to go with them. I couldn't tell if those were nostrils or airplane hangars. He was very overweight; he didn't need to go on a diet, he needed to go on a hunger strike.

His age was perfect: he looked as though his first job was parking covered wagons, and it was clear he hadn't bought any new clothes since the Nixon administration. He'd obviously replaced the lifetime battery in his watch about the time Elvis debuted on *The Ed Sullivan Show*. He was extremely hairy; after his audition, we referred to him as "Cousin It." I'd seen someone like him before, but I had to pay admission.

Not only was he physically perfect for the part, but his performance was terrific. He actually talked like a real person with human qualities (which I'll discuss in the next chapter). He was so believable, I knew at that point I had the right actor. It was one of those few times the character I had envisioned during the storyboard process appeared on tape. (For more discussion on a storyboard, see chapter 12.)

Unfortunately, during the playbacks his slate sounded like this: "Hi, I'm Bahhahoohoo and I'm with the Dewey, Cheatum, and Howe Agency." No one in the room understood his name. I said something to the casting director that is hardly ever said in an audition: "Could you please rewind and play that slate again?" When we're seeing so many people, no one in the room wants to repeat a slate. Everyone glanced at me like your dog looks at your answering machine when you phone and leave a message for yourself. It caused the type of frenzy that ensues when a cashier yells out, "This register is open."

So, by my request, the casting director rewound the tape. Again, I heard, "Hi, I'm Bahhahoohoo and I'm with the Dewey, Cheatum, and Howe Agency." He said his name so quickly that it was obvious he wanted to simulate time-lapse photography.

I again asked for a replay. The client looked at me like he was a gun dealer and I had just brought in a musket. Once again, I still couldn't understand the actor's name.

However, I did understand who his agent was. So I phoned the most prestigious agent in Hollywood and said, "John, it's Tom Logan. With regard to that international soft drink commercial, I'd like to sign 'Bahhahoohoo' to a three-year exclusive deal."

"Great! . . . I'm sorry, Tom, you'd like to book whom?" he asked.

"Bahhahoohoo," I replied.

"Tom, I have no idea who you're talking about."

"Neither do I, but I'm going to hold the phone up to the TV and play his slate back, so you can tell me who he is."

I did just that. This agent still couldn't figure out who his own client was. Since the commercial was to be shot only a day and a half later, I didn't have time to overnight the tape to the agent in Los Angeles, so his client lost the job. I have had this happen on more than a few occasions. *Make sure we understand your name.* Be sure to put plenty of separation between your first and last names. And keep in mind, this separation adds more time to your slate.

If you have a very strange name, or if the spelling is radically different from the way it sounds, it is sometimes advisable to spell out your name. Some of us are hooked on phonics and won't be able to find your name. If you don't like your name, then change it. I have a friend named John Lipshitz. He changed it—to David.

Be careful about giving abbreviations of your name that aren't the same as the name on your photo. If you slate your name as Cher, but on your photo you show your first name as Chernobyl, we will probably have a problem making the connection. And please slate your first and last name. For some reason, there are a few actors who apparently only have one name. If you're Cher, then fine, but all you other actors out there, please give us both your names. Models are the worst offenders when it comes to this practice. Why won't Dr. Phil give us his last name? He must be hiding something.

After the slate, be sure to pause for three or four seconds before you start reciting your commercial. There's a very quick discussion among the committee about each actor after he slates: "Wow, his nose is so big kids try to feed it peanuts"; "He's so large he influences the tides and Greenpeace might beach him"; "He's short, all right, but don't kid him about it or he might punch you in the knee." Also, some machines tend to roll the tape back slightly when we push the stop button. You don't want it to roll back just enough to cut off part of your name.

I used to take a stopwatch into auditions and actually time the discussions. The average discussion lasts 3.4 seconds. You don't want to be delivering your commercial during this discussion; we'll miss the beginning of your performance. All of this is assuming, of course, that we even watch your commercial playback.

Other Things We May Ask For in the Slate

When in an audition, listen very carefully to the instructions given to you. If it is the director giving you the information, this is his first indication of how well you do or don't take direction. Many actors are broadcasting when they should be listening. As a director I've learned something about listening: if I listen, I have the advantage, but if I speak, others have it. You win more friends with your ears than your mouth.

Although it is the exception rather than the rule, sometimes we may ask for additional information. Usually you are told what information we need from you before we roll the camera for your slate, so you should have a minute to collect your thoughts about what to say. However, there are times when we'll just ask you as the camera is rolling. This isn't a big deal, but just be aware that sometimes it does happen.

There are rare cases in which height or weight is so important for a particular commercial that we may ask you to state those statistics during your slate. Perhaps we are shooting a commercial with a famous basketball star, for example, and your height is important. Maybe we're shooting a commercial for a diet product and need to know your weight. Again, it is the exception that you'll be asked for this information, especially since we should already have it from your résumé, but don't let it throw you if you're asked.

There's a chance the auditioners will ask you for your age. By the rules of the Screen Actors Guild (SAG, the union having jurisdiction over actors in union commercials that are shot on film), this is illegal. It is also against all regulations of the American Federation of Television and Radio Artists (AFTRA, the union having jurisdiction over actors in union commercials that are shot on tape.)

Most people who ask you your age are just plain unaware of the regulation against asking. Very few clients know the rule and then purposely break it. If someone does ask, then give an age that is within the age range of the character for which you're auditioning. Usually your agent will have this information. If not, you'll probably get an idea of the age range for which they're looking when you read the script while waiting in the lobby.

Because of child labor laws we have a right to know, and it is perfectly okay for us to ask, whether you're under the age of eighteen. If an actor is a minor, it means that I have to hire extra people on a set to watch out for his well-being, and I am limited in the number of hours I can work him. So, for scheduling and budgeting reasons, we have a right to know whether you're a minor.

Age can sway opinions. Once I was directing a commercial for a hair product. We were looking for someone around twenty to twenty-five years of age. This one woman came in, and when the client asked her for her age, she stated that she was twenty-eight. After she left the audition, the client turned to me and said, "You know, she is absolutely perfect, but she's just too old." Look again at that sentence. Isn't it contradictory?

In fact, she looked young for her age, but she had planted in his mind the idea that she was too old because her age didn't fit the age range for which we were looking. He acted as though she was thirty when the West was won. I didn't contradict him because when he stared me down, I would've felt safer in the electric chair.

Weeks went by and we still hadn't found the right person. So I phoned this actress and told her to come back in and, when asked, tell us she was twenty-three. She was worried that the client would remember her age. I knew he wouldn't even remember *her*, much less her age, because we had seen so many people. I assured her that it wouldn't be a problem. I also politely asked her to dress a little more conservatively. I wouldn't say her bathing suit was skimpy, but I've seen more cotton in the neck of an aspirin bottle. And I told her that when she returned she needed to wear a bra—she had less support than Ralph Nader. It was apparent that her junior prom needed a day-care center.

Well, she did everything I asked her to. She came back to the audition and stated that she was twenty-three years old. Know what happened? You guessed it! After she left, the client turned to me and said, "Why didn't the casting director bring her in in the first place? She's obviously perfect for this part in every way—looks, character type, and age!" Correct me if I'm wrong, but hasn't the fine line between sanity and madness gotten finer? I used to think he was a pain in the neck, but I now have a much lower opinion of him.

Now, I don't advocate lying in an audition. About the only place an actor should fudge a bit is in the age department, if you're auditioning for a nonunion commercial. Again, in a union commercial you shouldn't be asked this question. Believe it or not, we usually know you're not telling the truth about your age and we're okay with that! Just be careful not to be so far off that it's obvious that you're deceiving us.

It is also against union regulations for us to ask your ethnicity. Again, if someone asks, usually out of his own naiveté, answer with whatever he's looking for, assuming it's believable given your appearance. You're thinking, "But Tom, you just said not to tell a lie in an audition, with the exception of age." Well, here's another area you can fudge—within reason!

During the slate, the auditioners might ask you to give them your profiles. Perhaps you're going to have to take a sip of the product for a soft drink commercial. The director knows that in the shot where you have to drink, you will be profiled so that the viewing audience will be able to see the label on the soft drink bottle.

If we ask for profiles, usually we want you to look directly into the camera for the name slate, then turn right and hold for a few seconds, and then turn left and hold for a few more seconds. Don't make the moves too fast. Depending on the camera and lighting, moving too fast could cause some blurring. And keep in mind that if you move too fast, we may not get to see what we need to.

Because it is possible that you'll be asked to show profiles in a slate, it's a good idea to do some checking of your back view before entering the audition room. Take a moment in the restroom to check your collar, primp your hair in the back, and so on. We've seen some pretty interesting things from the back. For instance, that toilet paper hanging from your pants isn't very becoming in an audition. I mention this because these types of things happen more times than you can imagine. When it comes to small problems like this, keep in mind that Murphy was an optimist. But please don't overdo it. We still want you to look like a real person, so you don't have to have every single hair in place. Some actors would want their X-rays retouched.

On rare occasions, part of the audition might consist of someone asking you to "tell us about yourself." In fact, the entire audition might consist of this question and your answer to it. An answer such as

"I have a slight gambling problem that sometimes leads me to theft" isn't appropriate. I don't like this question and I don't ask it on auditions. True, it helps some directors get an idea of your personality; as for me, I'd rather chit-chat *before* the taping to get that information. But be prepared for either situation.

A director may ask, "What have you been doing lately?" An answer such as "About what?" isn't appropriate. If a director asks you any version of these questions, I strongly suggest trying to stay away from talking about your acting credits. Keep in mind that we're seeing hundreds of actors, and at some point we're confusing everyone's list of credits. Think of it this way: if a hundred people verbally gave you their shopping lists, each consisting of five to ten items, you'd be pretty confused after the first ten. At some point, all lists begin to sound alike.

Keep in mind that we probably have your résumé in front of us anyway. Besides, in the commercial arena, having a lot of acting credits might be to your detriment. Many clients feel that actors who have a number of commercial acting credits are overexposed, and they worry that the public will recognize those actors from another ad. This would make their commercial seem less sincere. Remember, we don't want the public to think you're an actor. It could even be detrimental for you to have too many feature film and television acting credits on your résumé if you're auditioning for a commercial. Again, we're back to the problem of overexposure.

It would be better to show your personality by talking about other interesting things. For example, maybe you're a pilot and could talk about some interesting piloting experience. Maybe you're a snow skier and could talk about some interesting accident you had while on the slopes recently. Perhaps you could talk about some interesting showbiz story that doesn't include listing your credits. Hobbies, sports you play, a funny thing that happened to you on the way to the audition—all are examples of the types of things that interest most people in this industry. When meeting with a commercial agent, it would be more customary to talk about your credits; but even then, keep in mind that the agent probably has your résumé in front of her.

If you're in someone's office, look around the room to see what interests that person. I have pictures of my airplane and family on my desk. Anyone who starts talking about flying or kids has my attention. Perhaps the auditioner has photos of his dog hanging on a wall. People's offices can give you all kinds of clues about their interests.

Not having anything to talk about adds about as much strength to your interview as drop-kicking a wounded hummingbird. Be very confident. However, don't seem like the type that could add his head to Mount Rushmore, since it's already the right size. Don't overdo the chit-chat session. When there's nothing else to say, a bore is still saying it.

When I was young, way back in my acting days when I believed that June Lockhart really could understand what Lassie was trying to tell her, I used to do as much research as I possibly could on every person I auditioned for. It is much easier to do these days with the advent of the Internet, but even back then I could get research from other actors, my agent, and so on.

I once auditioned for a guest-starring role on a top-ten television show for ABC. I found out from friends that this particular director was into astrology. In fact, many people told me that he used astrology to help him cast his show. I know nothing about astrology. When it comes to astrology, if I spoke my mind, I'd be speechless. For all I know, my moon could be in Omaha.

I found out this director's birth sign and studied up on the subject. In the audition we started talking about astrology. In fact, he was so impressed with my knowledge on the subject that he figured I was perfect for the role. He gave me the part without even having me read. I guess it was in the stars. He was very weird. If he'd called the suicide hotline, they would have told him he was doing the right thing. Admittedly, this was a strange situation, but the principle of research applies to every audition.

Don't take this to the extreme. You don't want to come off as a phony. However, a little research on the person(s) for whom you're about to audition could go a long way toward meshing your personality with that of the auditioner(s). I can't stress enough the importance of having rapport with the people who are auditioning you.

Also, this chit-chat might give us some information about how you will or won't mesh with the crew. As the director, I have to judge whether your personality will fit with the personalities of the rest of the people who will be on that set. As you know, it only takes one individual to ruin a party! Actors tend to think that they are the most important people on the set. Keep in mind that the little wheels in the back of the watch are just as important as its hands.

As I mentioned, I prefer not to include this chit-chat session on tape, but some directors do. Frankly, when directors fast-forward through the slates, they rarely view more than five or so seconds of the chit-chat session anyway. This is one reason I don't like to include it on the tape.

For this reason and others, it is imperative that you not go on and on about yourself. Sometimes I'll watch a slate and realize that I've shot films in less time. While you're babbling on, I could go from Dr. Spock to Dr. Scholl's. Babbling is a sign of nervousness. We can't be sure which is knocking louder—opportunity or your knees. We'll soon realize that you have a fine personality, but not for a human being. It eventually becomes apparent that you're depriving a village somewhere of an idiot. Maybe we originally liked your approach, but now we want to see your departure.

Should You Slate "in Character"?

Many actors wonder whether they should slate "in character." The answer is no! I believe this is a major mistake. First of all, as I mentioned in *How to Eat and Act at the Same Time: The Sequel,* we don't always know what we're looking for. Nobody in the room agrees on what we're looking for. Whatever we're looking for, we'll change our minds anyway. So how could you ever figure out what we're finally going to settle on with regard to this character?

The problem is that if an actor slates while playing the character, then performs the commercial as that same character, we think that this is all he can do, and that he has no range as an actor. So unless you happen to guess exactly what we're looking for, we're thinking you can do only that one character. And even if you could slate with the character we're looking for, we'd still think you have no range.

You really are better served by slating as yourself. Even if the character is exactly "you," it is better to slate as yourself. You appear phony if you try to play a character while slating. If your personality happens to be a little different from that of the character, all the better. Then we'll see some range in your performance. Should you try to slate differently to show range if you are personally just like you perceive the character to be? No! I still say that you should slate with your actual personality.

Glasses and Slating

I'm often asked what an actor should do if he wears glasses. The simple answer is, "He should wear glasses." If you need glasses for reading and the lenses are thick enough to fry ants, then slate with the glasses off. This shows us how you look without glasses. Then put the glasses on to deliver dialogue while reading from a script. This will show us how you look with and without glasses, so we get to see two different looks.

If you don't need glasses, you might consider obtaining some "prop" glasses to be used for the slate. Go to your eye-care professional and ask him to provide you with glasses that contain plain nonglare lenses. This way you can slate with the glasses on and then take them off for the actual performing of the commercial. Again, you're showing two different characters. If we only see you with the glasses on, it's very difficult for us to see your eyes. Eyes that look like searchlights can distract a great deal from your face and performance.

I mention the glasses-off/glasses-on technique because frequently in an audition a client will say, "Let's see Jim again, and make sure he brings those glasses." Or I might hear, "Let's find out if he can move around without his glasses." In the latter case, the actor probably slated with them off and then put them on for the audition. Had that actor not slated without the glasses, the client might have never seen him any other way but with glasses and might consequently not have called him back.

Tail Slate/End Slate

Sometimes the auditioner(s) might ask you to "tail slate" or to do an "end slate." Both are just that—a slate at the tail end of your audition. The term comes from actual shoots. Often as a director I decide it would be more efficient to not reroll the camera, sound, and everything else between takes. So after the actors do a take, I might tell them to do it again and we'll "tail slate." (In this case, we're referring to an actual slate that contains the scene number, take number, etc.—discussed more fully in chapter 13.)

When we tail slate in an actual shoot, the person holding the actual slate will turn it upside down, so the stick will be banged up instead of down, and we'll slate it at the end, not at the beginning, of the scene. This informs the editor and reminds the director that all the information on the slate refers to the scene before, not after, the sticks touched.

Many times in auditions I'll ask the casting director to have the actors slate at the beginning of their audition and also to perform a tail or end slate. This way we don't have to rewind the tape to find out the name of the preceding performer, in the unlikely case that we watch his commercial in its entirety at a later time. It does make things go faster during the playbacks. Also, by doing two slates we're giving the actor two chances for us to understand his name.

After you finish your slate, don't forget the few-seconds-long pause I mentioned earlier. At this time you may see that someone in the room is half asleep. A yawn is at least an honest opinion. Don't take this too seriously, since the person in the room most likely won't be the actual person making final decisions. In fact, the odds are this person isn't the top dog. And even in the unlikely event that he is the decision maker, he'll have the option of watching your slate, and hopefully your performance, at a later time.

After the pause, you'll begin delivering dialogue from the script, which is the subject of the next chapter.

The Top Four Complaints about Your Performance

3

Even perfect people buy pencils with erasers.

Now that we've discussed the slate, let's get into what we look for when we do watch your actual performance. There are four complaints about actors' performances in commercial auditions that remain consistent year after year. These complaints, as I mentioned earlier, come from a compilation of comments from actual auditions that I've logged into a computer. In *How to Act and Eat at the Same Time: The Sequel,* I discussed the top complaints about you *personally.* In this book, I'll discuss the top complaints about your *performance.*

I will discuss the complaints in great detail, starting with the number 1 complaint. Interestingly, complaints number 1 and number 2 are also the top two complaints for actors' performances during auditions for television and feature film roles. Complaints number 3 and number 4 are unique to commercial acting auditions and/or actual commercial shoots.

Complaint Number 1: No Human Qualities

In this day and age, clients are more and more using "real people" (i.e., experienced actors who look and act like real people). The number 1 complaint I hear about your performance, be it in commercial, television, or feature film auditions, is "Tom, he has no human qualities." Ask a hundred actors what "human qualities" are. I bet you'd find that no more than three could give you a correct answer, but all of them are able to hum the theme song from *Green Acres*. Human qualities include all the quirky things people do when they're having a regular conversation. It's true that commercial dialogue isn't usually written in the style in which people talk in everyday conversation. But an actor must make it *sound* like normal conversation.

Frequently, a client will turn to me in an audition and say something like, "Let's send all of those actors home that are waiting in the lobby. They'll all sound like actors. Let's just go out and get real people, so they'll sound like real people." Ironically, many times "real people" sound more like actors than actors do! Maybe part of the problem is that many actors have spent years and years studying acting (which is a good thing) and now feel the need to use too much of the mumbo-jumbo they learned when it comes to performing in commercials.

Most of your actor training for other media will apply to commercial acting. But you have to be careful that you don't get so caught up in your acting method or technique that you forget the basics of just sounding like a real person. Ninety-nine percent of all actors in auditions read the lines perfectly, as though we want the character to sound like a robot. To explain human qualities, we'll use this following commercial:

I love Coke. Coke's great. I really want a Coke.

Read this commercial to yourself. Then put the script down and in your own words, *using none of the language of the actual script,* say out loud what the commercial says. I don't mean to do an entirely different commercial. I just want you to explain what the commercial states out loud as though you were talking to someone who doesn't understand it. In other words, I want it to sound as though you are just having a conversation.

So let's suppose you start off with, "Well, ahm, it just says that Coke is...." You just used a human quality. You said, "ahm." "But Tom, to say 'ahm' isn't professional." Wrong answer; I know my human qualities, Alex Trebek.

We don't want professional! Where did you ever get that idea? From some commercial acting class? You need that type of advice like newlyweds need *The Late Show*. The truth is, we want real people who talk and sound like, well, real people. (By the way, I'm including the human quality of "ah" along with "ahm." They are interchangeable.)

So let's go back to our commercial and add the human quality of "ahm." Now your delivery might sound something like this:

I love Coke. It, ahm, tastes great. I really want a Coke.

Now, I'm not talking about changing any dialogue whatsoever. "Ahm" is not a word. It's a human quality, and we want to add human qualities to the dialogue, not change it.

Again, say what the commercial says out loud and in your own words—as though you're talking to someone who doesn't understand the commercial and you're just explaining it.

So you say, "Well, it's about this Coke, that I...I really like and...." You just added another human quality. You hesitated or stuttered on a word. You said the word "I" twice.

"But, Tom, I can't stutter because I went to the Royal Shakespeare Theatre and I learned to talk like an actor." There you go again; your think-tank is leaking. You know what I think about that? I think it's beautiful. You speak perfectly—exactly like an actor. That's great. So when you're in the unemployment lines you'll be able to communicate with all the other actors who speak perfectly and are looking for work. We're not doing *King Lear,* we're selling Coke, for goodness' sake!

So let's go back to our commercial and add the human quality of a slight stutter or hesitation on a word.

The commercial may now sound something like this:

> I love Coke. It, ahm, tastes great. I . . . I really want a Coke.

Our commercial is slowly but surely beginning to sound like a real person talking. So let's continue. I ask you again to say out loud what the dialogue says in your own words. So you start off with, "Well, Tom, it, ahm, talks about Coke and . . . (*pause*) . . . how great it is. . . ." You just performed another human quality: you paused in the middle of a sentence. Do people actually do that in real life? *Absolutely!*

Pausing in the middle of a sentence is a human quality. Real people don't always talk in perfect sentences with no pauses in the middle. Only actors talk in perfect sentences—subject, verb, object, period, pause . . . subject, verb, object, period, pause. . . . No real human being actually talks this way.

So let's go back to our commercial and put in a pause somewhere other than at the end of every sentence. It might now sound something like this:

> I love Coke. It, ahm, tastes . . . (*pause*) . . . great. I . . . I really want
> a Coke.

Let's continue with our demonstration. Again, you start to describe the commercial in your own words: "Well, ahm, it's about this drink that . . . (*you laugh a little*) . . . that I really like. . . ." You chuckled! Laughter is a human quality. In real life, people will sometimes put in a slight chuckle as they speak.

So let's add a little laugh to our commercial:

> I love Coke. It, ahm, tastes . . . (*pause*) . . . great . . . (*little laugh*). . . .
> I . . . I really want a Coke.

Our commercial is really starting to sound like a real person talk-ing—not like an actor reading perfect dialogue to us. And—very important—we haven't changed one word of dialogue in the script.

Let's continue. Again I ask you to say out loud what the commercial says. Suppose you say, "Well, let's see, ahm...." You started to think. You paused a little to think of what to say next. Yep, you guessed it! Thinking is a human quality. And you know what? In real life, when people talk you can actually see them thinking of what to say next. It's only actors who read perfect dialogue with no "thinking process" whatsoever.

When I speak of the thinking process, I don't mean your eyes look up to the heavens for help. I don't mean "thinking" as an actor would when he can't remember his next line. I mean you, the actor, thinking as the character would think of what to say next. That's what people do in real life. The thinking process really makes it appear as though you haven't memorized a script and are just talking off the top of your head. Isn't that exactly what we directors want?

"But, Tom, the auditioners will think I don't know my lines and am having to think of what to say next." Right on. And while you're at it, please don't exceed the maximum effectiveness range of an excuse. I'm going to make you sound like a human being, okay?

So let's take our original commercial and add thinking process. Our commercial might now sound something like this:

> I love Coke. It, ahm, tastes... (add some thinking process here as you pause)... great.... (A little laugh here)...I...I really want a Coke.

I hope you're beginning to get the idea here. It's such a simple concept that we directors don't get why you actors have a hard time understanding it.

Let's continue the process. Let's say I ask you again to state in your own words what the commercial says. So you say, "Ahm, it's about this drink that tastes great. It really does and...." Let's suppose that you did not pause when you came to the period but instead you ran the two sentences together: "...that tastes great. *(No pause here)* It really does and...." Running two sentences together is a human quality. In real life people don't always stop at every period. However, actors frequently do just that.

So let's take our original commercial and run two sentences together. It might now sound something like this:

> I love Coke. It, ahm, tastes... *(add some thinking process here as you pause)* great.... *(A little laugh here as you run right into the next sentence without pausing)* I...I really want a Coke.

Getting the idea here? I must repeat, we haven't changed any dialogue whatsoever. All we're doing is adding human qualities. Next time you hear a conversation between two people in real life, listen to how they talk. They don't talk in perfect sentences. They don't put a perfect pause in between every sentence. They do have a *thinking process* sometimes as they speak. Sometimes they *pause* right in the middle of a sentence. Sometimes they have a quick *laugh* thrown in. They may *run two sentences together.* They may *stutter* or *hesitate* on a word. These are *human qualities,* and human qualities are what separate a real person speaking from an actor reciting dialogue.

I've only mentioned a few human qualities here. You'll hear thousands more if you really start listening to people as they talk. Real people, not other actors, will be your best resource as far as human qualities are concerned.

Now you're thinking, "But, Tom, this demonstration is unfair. Of course when you asked me to ad-lib the dialogue it sounded like a real person, because I was using my own words. But when I had to read from the script I was using someone else's words." Well, when you're delivering dialogue on the screen, to the public those *are* your own words. Therefore, they should sound as though you're just ad-libbing—talking off the top of your head—telling people from the heart how you feel about this product.

"But, Tom, this isn't fair, because I could sound more like a real person if I had the dialogue memorized." Really, you think so? When you have conversations in real life, do you have your speeches memorized before you talk to another person? You speak with many human qualities when having a spontaneous conversation. That's why you have human qualities: precisely because you are not speaking from memory.

"But, Tom, this seems like a lot of work." What, are you motivationally deficient? Actually, it's less work than acting. In reality, it's harder to be so perfect with your speech than it is to talk the way people actually talk in real conversations.

When I was an actor, way back in history before I was constantly thinking, "This food is a good source of fiber," I co-starred on a network television series. The star was a very well-known actor, and today he's a major star. He was telling us a joke. Just as he was getting to the punch line, the director called him to the set. This star yelled back to the director, "Hold up, I'm getting to the punch line."

"No, we need you right now," said the director.

This star ran over to the couch on the set and sat down. Literally two seconds later, the cameras were rolling as he gave one of the most incredible performances I've ever seen. He had tears flowing down his face as he was delivering lines about his deceased mother.

As soon as the director yelled "Cut," this star ran over to us and gave the punch line to the joke he had been telling before he was called to the set. I couldn't believe what I had just witnessed. So I said to this star, "That was great. The scene was so emotional. What were you thinking about during your performance?"

He retorted, "I was worried that the scene would take too long and that you wouldn't get the punch line."

"Oh, that's funny, sir. But I'm a student of the theater and would really like to learn your technique."

"That's what I was thinking about, sonny."

He went on to say that his "method" was not to learn the lines very well, so that when he delivered them the words would sound like they were just coming off the top of his head. (Sounds like human qualities to me!) He was serious. While I wouldn't recommend this method, he made his point. You have to make dialogue sound as though you are making it up for the first time.

Let's take another commercial:

> The other day I was hungry, so my mom took me to Burger Heaven for the first time. Boy, I will never forget it. They had this chicken sandwich that was so tasty, so delicious, so fantastic that I want to go back every day. So the next time you're hungry, go to Burger Heaven. You'll be glad you did.

Try this commercial using human qualities. Below is only one example of how you might make the commercial sound more real using human qualities.

Even before you say "The other day..." you could start off with a very slight laugh. I don't mean a big laugh, but a slight chuckle immediately before you start the commercial. That gets in a human quality before you even start the dialogue. After "The other day," you could pause slightly with some thinking process. So at this point the commercial would sound something like this:

(Slight chuckle) The other day *(slight pause, and think)* . . .

Next, let's put in a slight hesitation, maybe even a slight stutter, on the word "I." So now we have:

(Slight chuckle) The other day *(slight pause, with thinking process)* . . . I . . . I was hungry . . .

Again, let's put in a slight pause and some thinking process after "Burger Heaven." So we now have:

(Slight chuckle) The other day *(slight pause, with thinking process)* . . . I . . . I was hungry, so my mom took me to Burger Heaven *(slight pause, with thinking process)* for the very first time.

Next, after the word "boy," put in another slight pause and a chuckle, which brings us to this:

> (*Slight chuckle*) The other day (*slight pause, with thinking process*)...I...I was hungry, so my mom took me to Burger Heaven (*slight pause, with thinking process*) for the very first time. Boy (*slight pause with a little chuckle*), I will never forget it. . . .

Let's now run two sentences together, so that we don't have a perfect pause at the end of every sentence. We'll do this with the sentences "I will never forget it" and "They had this chicken sandwich . . . ." This brings us to:

> (*Slight chuckle*) The other day (*slight pause, with thinking process*)...I...I was hungry, so my mom took me to Burger Heaven (*slight pause, with thinking process*) for the very first time Boy (*slight pause with a little chuckle*), I will never forget it. (*No pause*) They had this chicken sandwich that was so . . . .

The commercial now seems to call for some thinking process as you rattle off the adjectives about how great their chicken sandwich is:

> (*Slight chuckle*) The other day (*slight pause, with thinking process*)...I...I was hungry, so my mom took me to Burger Heaven (*slight pause, with thinking process*) for the very first time. Boy (*slight pause with a little chuckle*), I will never forget it. (*No pause*) They had this chicken sandwich that was so (*pause, with thinking process*) tasty, so (*slight pause*) delicious, so fantastic, that I want to go back every day. . . .

Perhaps we can again run two more sentences together: "...that I want to go back every day. (*No pause*) So the next time you're hungry, ..." Now let's put in another slight pause, with thinking process: "... So the next time you're hungry (*slight pause with thinking process*), go to Burger Heaven." If we add a little chuckle here, we can finish off the commercial with a nice, warm human quality: (*Pause, with a slight chuckle*) "You'll be glad you did."

So, putting the entire commercial together, we might have something like this:

> (*Slight chuckle*) The other day (*slight pause, with thinking process*)...I...I was hungry, so my mom took me to Burger Heaven (*slight pause, with thinking process*) for the very first time. Boy (*slight pause, with a little chuckle*), I will never forget it. (*No pause*) They had this chicken sandwich that was so (*pause, with thinking process*) tasty, so (*slight pause*) delicious, so fantastic that I want to go back every day. (*No pause*) So the next time you're hungry (*slight pause, with thinking process*), go to Burger Heaven. (*Pause, with a slight chuckle*) You'll be glad you did.

Have you ever watched a commercial and thought to yourself something along the lines of, "Where'd they get that idiot wearing the loud pants and knit shirts with logos of animals on them, who's capable of getting lost riding an elevator? I could do that." That "idiot" is probably a professionally trained actor who is good enough at his craft to make you think we just grabbed him off the street and he's really telling us how he feels about this particular product.

Next time you're watching a television show or feature film, close your eyes and listen to how the actors deliver their dialogue. You're going to be amazed at how messed up it will sound to you. You will hear all of the above human qualities and thousands more. Also, listen to the *human quality sounds* people make while speaking naturally. You might hear, for example, a sigh, a grunt, or an intake of breath.

You've probably never noticed how *human* actors sound when you're viewing a television show or feature film. There's a reason: the dialogue was delivered so realistically, why would you notice? You'd only notice if someone talked in perfect sentences with no human qualities—like 99 percent of the actors who audition in Los Angeles and New York. Again, the actors you're watching in actual commercials are not making up their own dialogue. They are delivering it as written, since that's what ad agencies want. But they are adding human qualities.

Now, don't take this human quality thing to the extreme, being more "human" than people are in real life. You don't want too many of any one human quality in the same commercial. For example, putting in three "ahms" or "ums" in one commercial is a bit much. Using three stutters in the same ad is overdoing it and could make you sound so stupid you could forget your twin sister's birthday.

Use your good judgment. For instance, if you're a spokesperson for a company, then you might not want very many, if any, "ahms" or stutters. However, a chuckle, some thinking process, pausing in the middle of a sentence, running two sentences together, or something like that might be appropriate. Belching and passing gas, on the other hand, while considered an art form by my preteen sons, aren't the type of human qualities we need.

Even in a serious spokesperson commercial, which should sound *somewhat* professional, however, you should still sound like a real person speaking. No matter what the medium is, it would be rare for a director to want you to sound like a robot. Not many ad agencies want the viewing public to realize that we've hired an actor, not a real person, to do this job. We want the public to identify with the people in the ad.

To help you give a more natural delivery, take a tape recorder to all your commercial auditions. Arrive at the auditions early so you'll have a few extra minutes for rehearsal. When you get to the lobby, pick up the script, but don't sign in yet. Leave and go someplace private—your car, the park next door, anywhere you can be by yourself.

Read over the commercial a few times, but don't memorize it. Then put the script down and turn on the tape recorder. As I suggested earlier, just explain in your own words what the commercial says. In other words, act as though you are telling someone who doesn't understand the script what it means, as we did previously. You can start out with, "What the commercial actually says is…." Again, you're not doing a commercial here, just giving an explanation.

Then play back your recording. It will most likely sound very natural. I know what you're thinking: "Well, Tom, of course it sounds like I'm just talking and not acting, because when I talked into the recorder, I used my own words, but when I act I have to use someone else's words." I want to reiterate: the public should *think* you're using your own words. Therefore, your delivery of someone else's written dialogue should sound much like the way you talked into the tape recorder.

An excellent way to become a proficient cold reader with a natural style is to do the following exercise a few days every week. Take a magazine, newspaper, or anything you've never read before. Open it to any page. Look at the writing in any article you're seeing for the first time and start "saying," but not "reading," it aloud. Practice putting in the human qualities mentioned in this chapter, along with many of your own. Also, try opening magazines and looking for ad copy while performing the same exercise. Many ads in magazines have excellent ad copy (i.e., dialogue) for practice.

It won't take long before you become a great cold reader. The sad fact is, people who don't give good cold readings rarely get cast. There are very few actors who can't give good cold readings who are working in this business—whether the medium is commercials, television, or feature films.

Ironically, you have to work extremely hard to be phony. If I asked you to talk for thirty seconds about any subject you desired—school, work, lovers, for example—and told you not to use any human qualities (no chuckles, no stutters, no "ahms" or "ums," no pauses in the middle of sentences, putting a perfect pause at the end of every sentence, no thinking process, no hesitations on words, and so on), you'd have to work extremely hard at being phony to pull this off.

In fact, I've asked actors in classes for years to try to do this. They are amazed not only at how difficult it is, but that they can't pull it off at all. If you can't do it in real life, then it probably won't be believable on the screen. You just can't be that phony naturally. Being phony is hard work, and actors need to quit working so hard at it!

Let me reiterate an extremely important point. This doesn't mean you should ad-lib dialogue in the actual audition or, for that matter, in the actual shoot. You should stick to the exact words used in the script. The reason for having you ad-lib the example commercials was to emphasize how people talk in real life. If you mess up in an audition and add a word or two to give you time to find your place, no one is going to panic, but don't change the words in advance on purpose. In an actual shoot, if you change one word, it'll make everyone more nerve-racked than having an investigative team from *20/20* waiting in their offices.

I must remind you that even though you're using human qualities, your performance shouldn't sound sloppy. There's a huge difference between natural dialogue and sloppy dialogue. Your speech must be uneven enough to make it sound natural, but not so unbalanced that you sound dysfunctional. If you become so sloppy that it appears as though your only bath toys were an electric radio and a toaster, that's almost as bad as being so perfect that no one believes a word you're saying.

Changing Dialogue

Again, while tailoring your dialogue for a natural effect, be careful not to change the wording of the script. When you're actually shooting a commercial, for legal reasons you'll have to follow the script exactly, word for word. In the audition, a word or two that changed because you didn't know the script perfectly won't make that much difference, but you should still stick to the script. Remember, some ad executive(s) spent many hours on that script, and it was approved by dozens of people before it got to you.

Years ago I was directing a commercial for a major fast-food company. The actor was supposed to say, "Let's go get some breasts and wings." However, he had a hard time saying the word "breasts." He blurted out, "Let's go get some 'breasteses' and wings."

I immediately yelled, "Cut." I explained to him that the word was "breasts," not "breasteses." At first I thought he had perhaps just memorized the line incorrectly, since his glasses were thick enough that he could count molecules.

"Oh, okay, Tom, no problem," was his reply.

"And, action," I yelled, confident that we were now on the right track.

He again blurted out, "Let's go get some 'breasteses' and wings."

"Cut! Sir, the word is 'breasts,' not 'breasteses.'"

"Oh, Okay, Tom, no problem."

I then called out, "Action," thinking there was no way he was going to deliver that word incorrectly again. As has happened many times in the past, especially when I was married, I was wrong. He was definitely a fugitive from the law of averages. He just couldn't pronounce the word, period.

"Let's go get some 'breasteses' and wings."

This time I called "Cut" louder than I usually do. I didn't know how to fix the situation. I wondered . . . what would Scooby do? "Okay, forget it. You're going to get some 'wings and thighs,' okay?" I wanted to go easy on the poor fellow, who was so old he'd probably attended the First Supper.

"No problem," came his usual reply.

The commercial turned out great and everyone on the set was elated. I hadn't been that excited about anything since I had the dish company block Barney from my TV. To make a long story short, it's rumored that when the ad agency saw the footage in the editing room containing the word change, you could hear bomb explosions, blood-curdling screams, and reenactments of World War II.

Needless to say, it was a few years before I ever worked for that ad agency again. Bottom line: don't rewrite the script!

Chopping Words to Death

Another thing that drives us crazy that comes under the "human quality" heading is chopping the words to death. For some reason, many commercial acting classes teach their students to pound on every word—*chop, chop, chop.* No one actually talks this way in real life. If you watch local commercials, you'll hear this pounding on most words. Whether an actor is selling used cars, stereos, or Veg-O-Matics, you'll see extreme chop—especially in local markets. I'm sure there is a case to be made where the client wants chop and it would be effective. But 99 percent of the time it just sounds like an actor pounding on the words.

In real life people tend to kind of drag words out somewhat as they speak. Again, listen to people tell you about some product or movie they like. They won't chop the words to death. If you're in a commercial acting class that teaches you to pounce hard on certain words, you might want to reevaluate that class. Many commercial acting classes, especially outside the major markets of New York and Los Angeles, teach this style of commercial acting. However, it's sometimes taught in the major markets also.

Pitching Your Voice Too High

Almost all actors come into screen auditions (television, feature film, or commercial) and perform the material an octave higher than they really speak. If an actor pitches his voice much higher than his normal speaking range, he will begin to sound monotone in his delivery, not to mention like the star soloist in the Vienna Boys' Choir. If he's already speaking at the very top of his vocal range, he's not going to be able to make his voice go up for emphasis. Vocally, he has nowhere to go but down. If he would just talk at his normal pitch, he would be able to utilize all levels of his vocal range.

I believe this high-pitch thing comes from acting onstage. You have to talk a great deal louder when acting onstage, and this tends to push some actors' voices much higher in pitch than the level at which they would speak in real life. In other words, they have to project their voices to the last row in the theater to be heard. In the screen world, you rarely have to project as you would in the theater. The microphone is an inch above your head, with, most likely, another microphone under your shirt just below your mouth.

This is not to imply that your voice can't vary in volume. You should absolutely have variations in the loudness and softness of your voice. I'm only saying that the *pitch* of your voice should be within your normal vocal range, and that you shouldn't pitch it higher just because you're acting. Most actors do just that.

Now let's take our Coke commercial again. I want you to read the commercial ten times in a row, with no human qualities, while talking an octave too high and pounding the words to death. Do not add one human quality. Just read the lines perfectly, with a perfect pause at the end of every sentence but none in the middle of the sentence. Don't laugh, think, or hesitate on any words. No "ahms" or "ums." This will show you what we have to listen to when we view the final playbacks of commercial auditions.

Pretend that each sentence below is being delivered by a different actor. In other words, you're going to hear ten actors in a row during playbacks deliver this line:

> I LOVE COKE. COKE'S GREAT. I REALLY WANT A COKE.
> I LOVE COKE. COKE'S GREAT. I REALLY WANT A COKE.
> I LOVE COKE. COKE'S GREAT. I REALLY WANT A COKE.
> I LOVE COKE. COKE'S GREAT. I REALLY WANT A COKE.
> I LOVE COKE. COKE'S GREAT. I REALLY WANT A COKE.
> I LOVE COKE. COKE'S GREAT. I REALLY WANT A COKE.
> I LOVE COKE. COKE'S GREAT. I REALLY WANT A COKE.
> I LOVE COKE. COKE'S GREAT. I REALLY WANT A COKE.
> I LOVE COKE. COKE'S GREAT. I REALLY WANT A COKE.
> I LOVE COKE. COKE'S GREAT. I REALLY WANT A COKE.

Sounds awful, right? Now multiply those ten times by a factor of twenty. That's how many times I'm going to hear that commercial in that one day alone if I'm sitting through the original taping. Then, after we've heard that commercial pounded into our heads 150 times or more, one actor will walk into the audition and read it something like this:

> I love Coke. It, ahm (*add some thinking process here as you pause*), . . . tastes great (*a little laughter here as you don't pause and run right into the next sentence*)—I really want a Coke.

That actor will really stand out because he actually talked like a real person—unlike the majority of actors in an audition.

So when you're delivering the lines, forget those old reading inflections you used in high school when reading aloud. Forget the conventional rhythmic reading habits we all learned in those amateur acting classes. We don't talk that way in real life. Everyday conversation is quite different from regular reading. There's a different attitude in regular conversation than in reading. Talking is friendlier; reading tends to sound stilted and cold.

Projection

As mentioned in the "Pitching Your Voice Too High" section, the screen actor must remember that there is a microphone right above his head and usually one under his collar. We can even hear your stomach rumble, like Mount Vesuvius. Again, many actors who are accustomed to working on the stage tend to project very loudly because they are used to trying to hit the back row of the theater.

When working on camera, if you project as you would onstage, it will sound as though you're yelling. The audience (i.e., the microphone) is too close for that sort of thing. Now this is not to say that you should necessarily whisper, especially for a commercial. But keep in mind that you don't have to project your voice very far.

This is also not to say that your energy level should be low. Quite the contrary. Many commercials are bigger than life, and they demand much more energy than a similar real-life situation would. But don't verbally—or visually, for that matter—"push" beyond believability.

Yelling doesn't necessarily create energy. This is a screen medium, where less is more. Do you remember when your mom would get angry with you? When she used a very loud voice, it just didn't seem to have the same impact as when she was gritting her teeth and speaking very quietly but intensely. Women, if you really love a guy, which would have more impact: if he sent you two dozen roses, or if he sent you a single rose? If I have to have a child upset in a scene, which is sadder, many tears running down his face, or a smile and one slow tear falling from one eye?

Again, ask about the framing so you'll have an idea of how tight the shot is. This will give you some clue as to how much energy you need. Remember, the tighter the shot, the less physical energy is needed. However, the basic rule of thumb is, just do what you would do and speak the same as you would in real life under the same circumstances. Yes, you might be able to put a little extra spark into it since it's a commercial, but whatever you do, it still has to be real.

So if you have to whisper, then whisper—but do it as you would in real life, possibly with that little extra spark. Actors will sometimes say to me, "But I have to yell in this scene, so I can't do 'less.'" If you have to yell, then yell, but don't yell ten times louder than you would in real life just because you're acting. Yell as you really would if you were in that situation in real life.

Clients Are Baffled

At some point in every audition the client will turn to me and say something like, "Tom, is anyone going to come in here and talk like a real person talks?" And I'm going to answer, "No. Please don't count on it."

Then the client will say, "Well, let's just send all of these actors home and go out and find some real people because they'll talk like real people talk." *Wrong!* Believe it or not, real people usually talk more like actors than actors do. An individual client sits in on very few auditions because there is such a fast turnover in the ad agency business. They are usually amazed to find that actors all start to sound alike. This is one of the main reasons you should have human qualities in your delivery. The human qualities will separate you from the crowd.

Complaint Number 2: No Personality

It's astonishing to us that actors come into the audition with personality, leave the audition with personality, and have no personality between "action" and "cut." The minute I say "Action," something happens to the actor. He begins "acting." He no longer has the personality he had when he walked in the door.

Actors will come in smiling and joking with us. They'll be very friendly and talk like a normal person. However, once I mutter that magic word, "action," everything changes. Now everything sounds more formal and "actorlike." Next time you're in a commercial acting class and you're watching playbacks of your fellow actors, watch for this phenomenon. Notice that the moment the tape begins, the actor will be smiling and acting like a human being. Then the instructor will say that magic word, "Action," and you'll see that as the actor starts to slate, his face goes almost blank and he takes on a totally different persona. Most actors will lose their smile and their personality, and they'll stay lost for the entire commercial performance. Then notice that when the actor has finished his last line, and particularly after the instructor says "Cut," the actor will return to that friendly smile and again start acting like a normal person. In audition playbacks I can actually show everyone in the room the second an actor starts acting and the second he finishes acting, returning himself to a normal human being.

What's really interesting is that when an actor stops in the middle of his commercial to comment on the mistake he just made, he will talk to us like a normal person while describing his mistake, and then go right back to acting as he returns to the script. It's as obvious as the collagen in Angelina Jolie's lips.

In other words, it might sound like this:

> I love Coke, Coke's great, I, oh, I messed up there, sorry, I really want a Coke.

The most real part of this commercial performance will take place when the actor quits acting just long enough to tell us about her mistake—"Oh, I messed up there, sorry."

What's that all about? Why didn't the actor talk like a real person all the way through? It's because she was doing just that—acting. But she became a real human being when she quit acting. I know you're thinking that it doesn't make much sense to you for an actor to do this. If it makes you feel any better, it doesn't make much sense to us, either.

As we are fast-forwarding from slate to slate to slate without watching the commercials in between, how do you think we know when to stop the tape before we fast-forward into the next actor's slate? When the actor smiles and his face lights up and relaxes, we know he's through acting. We can actually see him going from an actor to a human being while in the fast-forward mode. Next time you're in a commercial acting class, ask the instructor to perform this fast-forwarding motion through actors' performances and you'll see exactly what I'm talking about.

As mentioned at the beginning of this chapter, the number 1 and number 2 complaints aren't just the two biggest complaints about actors auditioning for commercials. They are also the top two complaints about actors auditioning for feature film and television roles. However, the number 3 and number 4 complaints are exclusive to actors in commercial auditions.

Complaint Number 3: No Warmth

We covered warmth in the slate, but it also comes up as a complaint with respect to your performance. Often, when an actor starts acting, his face goes almost numb. Remember, this business is about friendliness. The audience has to like the actors in the commercial or it will not be a successful commercial.

Complaint Number 4: No Fun

Do you realize how many takes we're going to do of a national commercial during an actual shoot? We could literally do hundreds. No, we don't do that many takes because an actor keeps messing up. The fact is, because of union rules we have to pay the actors and the crew the same for an entire day's shoot as we would if they arrived on the set and we finished one second later. (In nonunion commercials, this may not be the case.) Therefore, many clients feel we should get the maximum amount of time out of you.

In other words, we might shoot many versions of any particular commercial. We might shoot you in different clothes for the same ad, different versions for each set of clothes, different versions for various regions of the country, and so on.

So if we feel you can't have fun performing the commercial in the audition (which is, in effect, take 1), what's going to happen when we're on a set and we're on take 40, or 50, or 100, for that matter? As a director I can tell you that as the day goes on, you usually don't get better. It would be extremely rare for an actor to have more warmth and believability on the fiftieth take than on, say, the fifth.

Making Mistakes

I can't write a book on our complaints about actors without including a section on apologies and mistakes. I won't write much about it here since I have a whole chapter dealing with this very topic in *How to Act and Eat at the Same Time: The Sequel*. But I just can't help myself. I need to say a few words about it.

First of all, when you make a mistake and continue your performance, we'll most likely just take that mistake for a human quality. Maybe you accidentally stuttered on a word. Maybe you lost your place so you paused in the middle of a sentence. Perhaps you made a small mistake and sort of chuckled. It's possible you weren't paying attention and didn't pause at the end of a sentence. You know, you could have lost your place in the script and had to think for a few seconds before discovering where you were in the script. I don't know about you, but to me all of the above look strangely like human qualities.

What drives us nuts is when an actor makes a mistake (and almost every actor does in an audition and in the actual shoot) and feels the need to stop, apologize, talk about the mistake, and then ask to start over again. You must realize that in an audition we're seeing hundreds of actors in a given day. The last thing we want you to do is start over. And, by the way, it is extremely rare for an actor who starts over to make the commercial any better the second time around.

So many times in an actual shoot an actor will make a mistake and I'll love it! Mistakes often make a performance look so much more real. However, if the actor stops and asks to start over again, it ruins that natural performance. This is very frustrating to directors. It's one of the primary reasons I grow hair everywhere but on my head; I'm usually pulling it out in auditions.

Although actors should follow the script word for word in an audition, you have to realize that just about every actor who auditions makes some mistake or other and drops or adds a few words. Of course, they all do it in different places. So, frankly, by the time we've seen a few dozen actors audition, the script is becoming a little hazy to us, too. However, this doesn't give you permission to rewrite the script.

When you mess up—and the operative word is *when*, not *if*—don't show us visually that you're messing up. Not only do actors talk about their mistakes, but they also feel the need to use facial expressions that show us they're messing up. They will pull the script up closer to their faces and squint their eyes as though the writer messed up or the script is hard to read.

We have no clue why actors do this, but it irritates us. In no other profession do people feel the need to tell everyone how poorly they are doing when they're trying to get a job. I can't imagine a doctor telling you what an incompetent surgeon he is just before putting you under the knife. Is this a doctor you would let operate on you? Nor can I imagine you interviewing a pilot to fly you somewhere if he told you in advance that he is nervous, incompetent, and makes mistakes. And I can't imagine the doctor or pilot, assuming you hired either of them, telling you about all the mistakes they're making while performing their duties. However, the majority of actors do just that in every audition they go on.

I can tell you, as a pilot myself, that mistakes are made in the cockpit as well as with air traffic controllers, ground control, control tower personnel, and, yes, other pilots, but pilots don't then turn to their passengers and talk about those mistakes. They don't make negative facial expressions and scrunch up their faces to emphasize just how awful the mistakes actually were while they're piloting the plane.

Again, I'm not going to go on and on about this, but I really hope you'll read chapter 1 of *How to Act and Eat at the Same Time: The Sequel.* I go into great detail about how actors apologize and the pitfalls to watch out for when they do make mistakes. Suffice it to say that you are going to make mistakes, you are going to mess up dialogue, and you are not going to be perfect (which we don't want anyway) in every audition you attend. Just do your best—the forest would be very quiet if no birds sang except the best singers. If you make a mistake, keep your cool, act like nothing happened, and just move on. As we will now do!

Commercial Dialogue

4

Advice from an old carpenter: Measure twice, cut once.

Many actors don't understand the meaning of the script they are performing. I freely admit that although I sing the song frequently, I don't know what a "Yankee Doodle Dandy" is. The same thing happens to actors when they're reading dialogue in auditions. They read along without knowing what they're really saying. Of course, sometimes trying to find the meaning in a commercial script is like trying to figure out the plot in a bowl of alphabet soup. Some of the writers' family trees are full of nuts. Then again, many people think of Shakespeare's plays as nothing more than a bunch of famous quotes thrown together.

This chapter deals with general concepts concerning commercial dialogue. The information tends to apply to the commercial audition more than to the actual shoot (though there's much overlap), because when you're actually shooting a commercial, the director will have many of his own ideas and concepts about the dialogue. The general rules that follow, however, will be extremely helpful to you in interpreting dialogue, which will aid you in winning commercial roles.

Many products that are advertised on television are not in and of themselves exciting or even mildly interesting. The ad agency is in charge of the script, but it's my responsibility as a director and your responsibility as an actor to present the product in a unique and interesting way. Even the most common, mundane article can be transformed into an appealing product.

One important concept to learn is that it's not only what you say, but how you say it. For example, the phrase "Excuse me" really isn't that funny. But when Steve Martin says "Excuuuuuuuuuuuse *me!*" he gets a gigantic laugh. Words by themselves, like lines, generally aren't what get the laugh or the meaning across. The same is true with commercials. The actor, by his interpretation of the dialogue, will or will not get the message(s) across to the public.

When I was an acting instructor, way back when the Grand Canyon was just a hidden valley, I employed an interesting exercise that emphasized how an actor can deliver a line that means nothing and make it mean something. I would tell two students to go outside the classroom and discuss a scene they'd like to show to the class. They would decide on a location, whom they're going to play, what their relationship to each other would be, and so on. When they came back into the room, I would give them two telephone books to use as scripts.

They had to read directly from the phone book but put in all of the inflections and human qualities, everything they would have had to put in had they been saying the actual lines of a script. If the two did a good job, the other actors in the class would be able to discover what was going on in the scene. The point is, the two actors were getting their message(s) across to the audience purely through their delivery and visual reactions to each other, which I'll discuss in more detail in chapter 8. Their interpretation of the lines was more important than the actual words used in the script.

When interpreting lines, actors can fall into either of two obvious traps: overplaying or underplaying. Putting too much emphasis on the words has the same effect as reading a book with every word capitalized or italicized; since everything stands out, nothing does. Pound hard on every word and it's a sure bet the message will be lost.

What makes something stand out is its differences from the other parts of the script.

While trying to avoid overplaying, many actors sometimes put too little emphasis in their interpretation. Their performance then becomes lackluster and dull—and that certainly isn't going to sell anything! Commercial acting takes a lot of energy.

The sections below will explain the major points you need to learn with regard to interpretation so that your performance will be as effective as possible. The divisions I have chosen will help you review the major elements individually, but keep in mind that they do overlap and relate to one another.

Types of Commercials

Spokesperson Commercial

There are three basic types of commercials, each with subtypes. The most basic type of commercial, and the oldest, is the *spokesperson* commercial. A spokesperson commercial is just that: someone speaking for the company. The spokesperson commercial usually consists of one actor looking directly into the camera talking about the great qualities that a particular product possesses.

This is the most formal type of commercial. It was the first format television advertisers used, and it is the most simple and direct. Although beauty was the norm when television commercials first began, the types of people cast in spokesperson commercials have become somewhat more varied. In this day and age, you could see, for example, a weird car or carpet salesperson who's more animated than *The Simpsons*. The extreme spokesperson commercial (one with a "far-out" character type) is used more on a local level than on a national one, but that's not always the case.

The following script is an example of a spokesperson commercial:

> WOMAN: I work long, hard hours. When I come home, I want to
> sleep like there's no tomorrow. And, because of Lear mattresses,
> I can do just that. See, Lear mattresses have an extra patented
> layer that no other mattress has. It's no secret that we call it "the
> extra pad." So, if you're looking for a good night's sleep, check out
> "the extra pad" from Lear mattresses. You'll be glad you did.

Slice-of-Life Commercial

One of the more common types of commercials used today is the
slice-of-life commercial. This is just what the name implies: you are
seeing a part of supposedly real life. For example, you might see a
married couple sitting at the breakfast table discussing their terrific
coffee. A small "story," usually one that has more than one character,
is being shown to you. Below is an example of a slice-of-life commercial script.

VIDEO	AUDIO
A HUSBAND is sitting at the break-fast table reading the newspaper.	HUSBAND: Honey, where's my coffee?
His WIFE sticks her head out of an interior kitchen door.	WIFE: It's coming. I have a special treat for you.
The wife's head disappears behind the door.	HUSBAND: I just want my usual coffee.
The wife enters the room with a coffee cup and server on a silver platter. The husband notices the presentation.	HUSBAND: Hey, what's the occasion?
The wife pours the coffee for her husband and puts the cup in front of him.	WIFE: It's just your "usual coffee."

The husband takes a sip.	HUSBAND: My "usual coffee" tastes different. *(pause)* Wow, what makes it taste so much better?
The wife puts her hand around her husband's shoulders.	WIFE: The brand. It's new—Baron's coffee.
They both smile at each other.	HUSBAND: It's so delicious!
The wife kisses her husband on the forehead.	WIFE: And so are you!

As this cheesy example demonstrates, we are seeing a part of this married couple's life, hence the term *slice-of-life* commercial.

Narrative/MOS Commercial

Narrative/MOS commercials, in which no dialogue is being delivered by the actor(s) actually seen in the commercial, are being used more and more. The "narrative" part is obvious: someone is narrating the commercial. The letters "MOS" are a little more mysterious. You'll often see these letters not only in commercial scripts, but also in television and feature film scripts.

Many people in the industry believe that "MOS" stands for "mitout sound." In fact, that has become more or less the accepted belief among many industry professionals. When German filmmakers first came over to America to make movies, they would commonly say, "Let's shoot this scene mitout sound." *Mit* is German for "with," and "mitout" is a kind of Gerglish (the German version of Spanglish) for "without." So as a kind of tribute (or knock—no one is really quite sure which), many industry people started saying "mitout sound," meaning there would be no audio recording during the shooting of a particular scene.

Many sound mixers will tell you that "MOS" stands for "minus optical sound." Other sound mixers will say that "MOS" actually stands for "minus optical stripe." (The optical stripe is the stripe you see on the sides of filmstrips that carries the sound information.) I've even heard people say it stands for "mixer out smoking" or "mixer out stoned." But I think it's safe to say that you can rule out the latter two.

Whatever MOS stands for will be debated forever, but the bottom line is, the meaning is the same: there ain't no sound being recorded during the actual shooting.

In scripts you will commonly see, for example, a phrase such as, "Woman washing kitchen counter (MOS)," or "Man walking down the street (MOS)." There are many reasons sound may not be needed. Chief among them would be if music is utilized instead of dialogue spoken by the actors.

The narrative/MOS commercial has become more common since the advent of music videos, since almost all music videos are shot MOS. In fact, many commercials now resemble music videos because they are so popular these days. Commercials follow trends. When cowboy movies are popular, for example, you'll see commercial styles follow suit.

If asked to do an improvisational MOS commercial, it's important that you have a beginning, a middle, and an end. The task is usually very simple. Suppose the commercial is for a tile cleaner. Your instructions from the director might consist of something like, "Okay, we need to show how great our cleaner is. So you need to show that it doesn't take much rubbing to get those terrible stains off the tiles."

The beginning might consist of you looking disgusted as you view the stains on the tiles. You could show on your face that you think nothing will get these tiles clean. The tiles are so dirty that even your shockproof watch is embarrassed. They're dirtier than young female pop singers who resemble strippers.

For the middle, you could begin to wipe with the miracle cleaner. You just barely wipe, then look at your rag as if you can't believe how dirty it is. Then you glance down at the counter and are amazed at how all the stains have been removed.

For the ending, you could pick up the product, look at it, smile, and shake your head up and down for a "yes" response. You are ending on a positive note, which is a very important aspect of any commercial.

Some actors' improvs are so long that they become miniseries; I've shot movies in less time. Doing this kind of improv is a huge mistake. At some point in an extremely long improv, the actor simply starts to look silly. When your improv drags on and on, we begin to realize that perhaps you got into the gene pool when the lifeguard wasn't looking. We'd just as soon watch the Weather Channel. Keep in mind that an entire commercial is almost always less than thirty seconds long; you don't need to create an epic here. It's important not only that you get across the point on a positive note, but that you do so in a timely manner.

When directions are given to you to do an improv in an audition for this type of commercial, listen very carefully. The directions are usually very specific, since the director already knows what is called for in the script. Too many actors nod their heads up and down and aren't really listening. We usually chalk this up to nerves, but we also realize you might be just as nervous, or maybe even more so, during the actual shoot. When you don't adhere to our directions, you begin to look like the type that watches the Three Stooges and takes notes. You make us feel at home, even though we wish we were.

If you don't understand some direction, by all means, ask for clarification. Sometimes our directions are obscure. We might not have all of our dogs on the same leash. So it is perfectly acceptable, even advisable, to ask for clarification. But don't ask us how to play the part. Don't ask us what you should do in the improv. You're the actor. We expect you to have some imagination. A doctor doesn't ask you how to perform surgery. When I board an airplane, I don't expect the pilot to ask me how to fly that heap of metal.

Below is an example of a narrative/MOS commercial.

VIDEO	AUDIO
A MAN is scrubbing tiles in a shower.	NARRATOR: Do you hate cleaning those scummy tiles in the shower?
The man is becoming more and more frustrated. He begins to scrub harder and harder.	Do you have better things to do than to exercise your biceps on the shower tiles?
The man is now scrubbing so hard his hands are just a big blur on the screen. (SFX)	Then you need the new Scrub-a-Way cleaner from Baron & Company.
ECU of Scrub-a-Way bottle.	It's fast and effective and requires oh-so-little scrubbing.
The same man is now sleeping in his bed, happily snoring away.	Your dreams can come true, too, by purchasing the new Scrub-a-Way— at supermarkets everywhere.

Although a narrative/MOS commercial obviously has no sound recorded during the actual shoot, this is a good place to mention improvising dialogue. Years ago, back when a "crack salesman" meant the guy was great at what he did, clients would ask actors to come into auditions and improvise dialogue. Many times this was because the client didn't yet have a script and wanted ideas. Sometimes the actors became their scriptwriters.

In a union commercial audition, if you're asked to improvise dialogue you are supposed to be compensated in the amount of $212.50. In the SAG Basic Agreement that companies using SAG actors in commercials sign, this is referred to as a "Creative Session."

Commercial Styles

There are various commercial styles you'll frequently hear discussed by your agent. Styles have to do with how you are to dress, among other things. The style of the commercial also affects how you say and interpret the dialogue.

Obtain all the information you possibly can about the commercial before going to an audition. And no matter what type of clothing you wear to a particular audition, always pack a few extra styles in the trunk of your car. If you're in New York City, then have extra clothes stuffed in a briefcase or tote bag.

Many times you will show up totally wrong in the style department. By the time your agent obtains the information about the commercial, it has been passed down from the client to the director, to the producer, to the casting director, to your agent, and then to you. All of these people will have given the information their own twists and interpretations. So by the time the information gets to you and you interpret it, it could be totally off base.

The basic styles are as follows:

Character

Frankly, this is the category most actors fit into. Character types are used in commercials much more than beauty types. The connotation denotes someone who might be a little out of the mainstream. The dress code could be just about anything, depending on the type of character.

For instance, a hippie-style, 1970s-era person so poor he keeps food stamps in his money clip would dress and deliver dialogue differently than a balding grandfather type who has a picture of Moses in his school yearbook. The age group could range from anyone who was just born to someone older than all of those people over a hundred whose photographs appear on Smucker's jars.

Character types might have strange hair, for instance, that makes it look as though a porcupine climbed up on their head and died. If your beehive hairdo was ruined by a ceiling fan or if your eyebrows resemble azalea bushes, you're probably in the "character" category. Someone who is overweight and could be a stunt double for Shamu would also be considered a character type. Included in this category might be someone so nerdy he makes Mr. Rogers look cool. You can see that this category runs the gamut.

Casual

The term "casual" implies that you should dress and "be" as it states— casual, or just dressed in regular clothes. Nice jeans or casual slacks are appropriate here for both men and women. This information definitely doesn't mean for you to dress like a professional. It tells you that your character might be a regular Joe and that you should dress, and probably even act, with that in mind. You could be anything from the type that was born in a log cabin to the type that was born in a manger. The typical *casual* type male might, for instance, be the type that loves to watch girls exercise on television and would consider Pamela Anderson the perfect wife.

Some actors take this category to mean sloppy—the type of person who thinks Slim Jims and Moon Pies are two of the basic food groups. You're dressing too sloppily if you dress in clothes that would get you fired from a construction job due to your appearance. Usually, casual doesn't imply a homeless person! If we want sloppy, we will tell you so. The sloppy look is rarely used in commercials. In fact, it's used so little that we don't even give it its own category.

Upscale Casual

"Upscale casual" is taken to mean a nicer style of dressing than casual, but still not too dressed up. It designates nice slacks for men, and possibly a nice dress for women. This dress style doesn't designate the professional type of person, but it also isn't as low-key as casual.

Business/Professional

This term denotes, for example, a doctor, banker, lawyer, or some other type of professional person. For men, this usually means wearing a business suit. An upscale dress, for example, might be appropriate for women. Dressing in casual clothes for this type of commercial makes about as much sense as Noah letting Chia pets aboard.

Again, it is imperative that you carry other styles of clothing with you to an audition other than the style you are wearing when you arrive. After you read a script, you might be shocked to find that it requires a totally different style than the one originally described to you. Also, keep in mind that people on the committee change their minds a lot. It might be that the committee changed the style of the commercial the day of your audition and none of the agents were informed. When the committee more or less reaches agreement on an idea, it's kind of like being married to Larry King: you know it's going to be painful, but it won't last very long. The committee members might not have ulcers, but they're carriers. I've learned that it's best to feign deafnesss during these meetings.

Analyzing the Script

It's important for you to realize from the outset that there is no right or wrong way to interpret a script. Some ways might be more appropriate than others and some may work better than others, but everyone who auditions will interpret the script differently. That's a good thing!

When we're seeing as many people as we do for a commercial audition, we're thrilled to see different interpretations. After all, if everyone interpreted the script the same, we wouldn't need to have actors audition. We would just have to look through photos and find the right look, and our casting job would be over. Fortunately, this isn't the case. If you go see Hamlet performed in ten different productions, you'll see ten totally different versions of the character.

The important thing is, make choices and stick with them throughout your performance. Even if your choices are wrong, that's okay. I can fix a bad choice. What I can't fix is a reading that is all over the place because the actor hasn't committed to his interpretation of the character.

For instance, let's say you decide that the character for which you're auditioning fits into the "character" category and you decide to play him as a surfer bum. Maybe the script didn't call for that, but you just thought it sounded reasonable after reading the script. This is a choice, which may or may not be a good one, depending on the situation. Let's say that I, as the director, decide that a surfer bum is way off base for this particular character. I can easily ask you not to play it as a surfer bum. But if you make no choices, I really don't know what to change. I can direct something that is wrong (at least in the eyes of those judging the audition), but it's extremely hard to direct nothing.

So it's okay, and possibly advisable, to try something unique with the character as long as it stays true to the character and the message the client is trying to put across. And, since the odds of your getting this job are always pretty slim, you might as well go for it—within reason. A turtle never makes any progress until he sticks his neck out.

Not only does an actor need to know the type and style of commercial for which he's auditioning, but it's also very important for him to understand what he is saying in a commercial. How can you interpret dialogue from a play, for example, if you don't know what the character is supposed to get across? The same is true with commercials. You should examine the script closely enough to fully understand the purpose, or message, and the meaning of each sentence as it fits into that purpose.

At the same time, be careful not to analyze the script to death on a commercial audition. Once you've decided how you are going to get the meaning across, I'd avoid trying to figure out which words to emphasize in every sentence, or you could lose the natural flavor of the script.

Many times on my sets I will hear actors in their dressing rooms working on their scripts. They'll take a particular sentence and read it over and over again, emphasizing a different word each time. For instance, if an actor has to say the line "I think you're a jerk," I might hear that actor in his dressing room performing a ritual: "*I* think you're a jerk. No, that's not it, let's see.... I *think* you're a jerk. No, that's not it, either. I think *you're* a jerk. Not there yet. I think you're a *jerk*. It's just not sounding right. Let's try this: *I think you're a jerk*."

This actor is beating the line to death. Why can't he just look at the character to whom he is speaking and simply say, "I think you're a jerk"? Sound too simple? That's the point. Actors often make their jobs much harder than they really are.

Now, it is true that by changing the emphasis from one word to the next, you totally change the meaning of a particular line. Let's take the sentence "I'm going to the park." It seems like a simple enough sentence with a direct meaning. If you change the emphasis from one word to another, however, the sentence takes on new meanings. For example:

◆ "*I'm* going to the park." This means that *I* am going and not you or anyone else.

◆ "I'm *going* to the park." This means that you aren't going to stop me; I'm *going* anyway, no matter what you say or think.

◆ "I'm going to the *park*." This means that I'm going to the *park* and nowhere else.

You can see from this demonstration that you can take a sentence and, by changing the emphasis from one word to another, get a new sentence with a whole new meaning. The way to handle this in a commercial audition is to just say the words while keeping in your mind the meaning behind what you're saying.

Of course, you do this in real life. You don't think to yourself, "Now I'm going to tell him that I'm going to the park and the emphasis should be on the word *going.*" You're concentrating on the fact that you are going to tell him you're going to the park and that no one can stop you. And when you say that sentence, you'll deliver it with the right emphasis—"I'm *going* to the park."

Your performance will become stilted if you concentrate solely on the words to emphasize instead of the meaning of what you're trying to get across to the other person. It's apparent that words have many meanings. The trick here is to try to be honest with the material—unlike, say, Barry Manilow, who *didn't* write his hit song "I Write the Songs."

Comedy versus Drama

There is a very fine line between acting for comedy and acting for drama. Many married people will tell you there's a fine line between love and hate. If it's supposed to be a humorous commercial, a great many actors make the mistake of coming into an audition and pushing to play something funny. When an actor tries to be funny, it usually comes off very forced, especially in the screen media.

Have you ever been in an acting class where one of your fellow students played a scene so dramatically that it actually became funny? Bingo! That's because usually something becomes funny if it's played too seriously. For instance, watch any really well done sitcom. (Is that an oxymoron?) Notice that the characters are very serious. That's what makes them funny.

So, in an audition that is supposed to be humorous, be careful not to try too hard to make it that way. The bottom line is, just be true to the material. The humor will come out if you play the humorous piece very seriously. Most actors do just the opposite. Then again, most actors aren't on the callback list.

One-Liners

Believe it or not, a single line can be much more difficult to handle than a whole block of dialogue. Ask actors who have acted onstage, for instance, whether it is harder to deliver one line in a play or a few dozen. The problem is that you just don't have much to go on when it comes to how to say that one line. Many times that one line just seems to come out of nowhere.

Also, when an actor has only one line, that line becomes terribly important to him. And it is important to us, or we wouldn't have put it in the script in the first place. Every actor on a set costs us money. Our liability insurance premiums, for instance, rise with the number of people on a set. Our food costs rise, as well as the cost of dressing rooms, the need for more make-up and wardrobe personnel, and on and on and on. None of this, of course, includes the cost of the actor, his overtime, meal penalties, wardrobe calls, pension and welfare, health insurance contributions, and, most important, all the re-use fees he will be receiving for each airing from now through eternity. The list of costs goes on and on.

So if an actor only has one line, it is important to us. However, often actors make their one line the most important line in the entire commercial. In other words, they practice that one line so many times that it no longer sounds natural. In a commercial audition, if your part consists of one line only, it is fairly common for us to ask you to perform a few different interpretations of that line. So if you show up for a commercial audition and realize you only have one line, then it would behoove you to practice it with at least three different interpretations before you're called into the actual audition room. After all, in the actual shoot the director will want many different deliveries so he and the client can choose the perfect one (at least in their eyes) for the final version. Of course, as you now know, there will be absolutely no agreement among the committee members on which interpretation is best.

Also, we may shoot different versions of that line for different parts of the country. For instance, you might be dressed up in a cowboy outfit for the southern version, a business suit for the northeastern version, and beach attire for the West Coast version. The delivery of that line would most likely be different for each area.

Usually, however, unless otherwise instructed, you don't need to perform the one line with different accents or dialects, as I'll discuss later in this chapter. But we do want different interpretations to portray different ideas. As seen with the "I'm going to the park" example, one can get many interpretations out of a few words of dialogue.

There is an even greater tendency to try to find the right word(s) to emphasize when you only have one line. Again, actors will beat it to death. But instead of taking that one line and emphasizing a different word each time, why not think of the meaning behind the line and then just say it as you would in real life? This way the meaning comes from within, not from artificially punching a word while delivering a particular line.

For practice, try different interpretations with the following one-liners:

◆ "Susie, you look so vibrant today."
◆ "What do I drink in the morning? Daffeny's Coffee."
◆ "Let's clean up America."
◆ "The taste is out of this world."

Marking the Script

When an actor begins to look over a commercial script, I think it's a bad idea to underline words and mark up the script. But this is strictly a personal belief. If I tried to follow the marks on a page, my delivery of the commercial dialogue would sound very rehearsed and phony. It might be right for *you* to mark the script, but be careful that you don't think you have to follow those marks each time you rehearse it. If you do, then you're going to fall into the rhythmic patterns I discussed earlier.

In everyday life we don't deliver the same sentences the same way each time we use them—even if the situation is somewhat the same. We let words flow freely. This is the natural quality that we directors look for in commercial actors during auditions.

We get pretty bored in auditions, so we tend to play little games. One game we play is "Bet Which Words the Actor Underlined on the Script." (Of course, if the actor chooses to use a cue card, our game is over.)

After the actor leaves the room, we take turns guessing which words each actor underlined. Since each actor leaves his script behind when he departs, we tally up which words the actor underlined in the script to see who won that particular round. Amazingly, we're pretty close to a perfect score each time. It is so obvious to us which words you think you need to pounce on. In my opinion, anyone who tells you to mark the script is not giving you a very smart suggestion and is the type who, when he opens his mouth, it's only to change feet.

Let me repeat: it is better to just say the line with the intent behind it so the right words will be emphasized naturally. Right before you're about to yell at someone, do you actually stop and take the time to work on which word(s) you're going to emphasize? No, you just say what you have to say with the right intent and it all comes out sounding fine.

meaning behind the lines without concentrating on each specific word in the script. Try to come up with a visual image (or set of images) that represents your personal interpretation of the message.

Now pick up the script and say those lines of commercial dialogue, keeping that picture in mind. You'll notice a change in your speech. The "color" of the image will naturally show up in the appropriate word or words. This is the way the commercial should sound.

Again, don't spend too much time on this or you'll end up over-analyzing the dialogue. I mention it only as a guide to how your commercial should ultimately sound. This is why using a tape recorder before you go into the audition room is so important. When you play back your commercial, you should hear the "color" in the words.

Transitions

By concentrating on the meaning of what you're saying as opposed to the individual words, you'll observe transitions. In everyday conversation, we naturally group together words and ideas that belong together. Our voice and attitude automatically change when we move from one thought to the next. That thought change could come at the end of a sentence or in the middle of one.

As an example of a typical transition, let's take the following: "Susie, you're so sweet. Thanks so much for the present. Oh, did you get mine?" You can see the obvious change of attitude (transition) from "Thanks so much for the present" to "Oh, did you get mine?"

Transitions occur constantly in everyone's speech, so look for them. Be sure to use transitions when reading commercial dialogue so your delivery will appear natural. Not only does dialogue sound unreal when transitions are missing, it also becomes very boring. Thoughts aren't separated when you're just reading dialogue, so ideas all sound the same. Remember that when everything sounds the same, nothing stands out.

Try delivering the following sentences with transitions. The slash (/) denotes a transition.

- "XYZ coffee tastes great. It's the absolute best. / It's available right now at your local supermarket."
- "We're talking to Jill Forman of San Diego, California. / Jill, why do you like Poppity-Pop popcorn?"
- "Kate, I smell something good. I hope it's what I think it is. / Oh, you shouldn't have."

Asides

Asides are used frequently in commercials. They are words spoken in supposed secrecy. Usually, they are spoken directly to the camera and therefore directly to the audience, but there are exceptions. For example, a commercial may go something like this:

> (*Actor looking right into camera*) Hey, everybody! Have I got a surprise for you! You should get the new Bald-Away spray product. Just one spray on the head and presto, you have hair. It's great. It really works. Look at the top of my head! (*Secretly to the audience with a lowered voice*) It used to be bald!

An aside is a very effective tool to use for communicating personal thoughts and ideas directly to the audience or your on-camera partner. You'll see many examples of asides in commercials. It should be obvious to you by now that they require a transition.

Pacing the Copy

Though you should have energy while delivering the dialogue, *don't rush the copy!* Actors tend to get nervous and run through the dialogue too quickly, and then they rush out the door and are off quicker than the babysitter's pink dress. You can probably remember giving a speech in high school that was supposed to be, say, five minutes in length. You practiced at home and it came out to five minutes and ten seconds, another time five minutes and three seconds, and so on. When you got up in front of the class, however, it came out to about three minutes because you were speaking at 150 words per minute, with gusts up to 190.

We must give the audience time to let our message sink into their brains. The nervous actor tends to run all the words and sentences together so quickly as to not give the audience time to digest what has been said. The performance looks phony because the performer isn't taking the time to collect his thoughts; people usually take a little time to think of what they're going to say next. (Remember the chapter on human qualities!)

Whatever you do, don't have the same pacing throughout the script. Again, we get back to how real people speak, as opposed to actors who are reading dialogue. When we read, we tend to keep the same pace throughout, making the commercial drag. However, in everyday conversation, we tend to speed up a little, then slow down, then speed up, and so on. It's the irregularity of the delivery that gives it that human quality and keeps it from being monotonous. It's not going fast that keeps the pace interesting; it's going at an irregular pace.

If you say the *entire* commercial very slowly, nothing stands out. However, if you're clipping along at a normal rate and then slow down to say, for instance, the product name, then the product name would stand out since it is being delivered at a different pace than the rest of the commercial. The opposite is also true.

It is true that speeding the pace up a bit can add energy to a stage play. Many times you'll hear a stage director say something like, "Pick up the pace. I can drive a Mack truck through those lines. Pick up the cues." Keep in mind that stage acting is an auditory medium. How fast or slow the actors deliver their dialogue and pick up their cue lines sets the pacing for the entire play.

However, television shows, feature films, and commercials are visual genres. You, the actor, do not really set the pace. Pacing is set more in the editing room by the editor, and ultimately by the director, than by the actor. How quickly the images move onscreen will determine the pacing. For example, watch some music videos. It's not so much the singer who moves the scene along (that is, determines the pacing) as it is the images that move that scene.

Suppose we have a scene where a guy slowly walks over to a car, patiently gets into it, and hesitantly drives off. This scene, in and of itself, doesn't "move" very fast. However, let's say that I cut to an extreme close-up of feet walking. Then the screen cuts to a close-up of a very determined face. Next, I cut to an extreme close-up of a hand opening a door. Next comes a series of extreme close-ups: the key going into the keyhole, a foot pushing down the accelerator, the tachometer and speedometer needles jumping, a smile on the driver's face, exhaust coming out of the exhaust pipe, the wheels spinning in the dirt, and so on.

All of a sudden this scene is really moving. It's not so much the action that makes the scene move as it is the visual. Two people just standing there talking may not move a scene, but quick cuts back and forth of close-ups of the actors and to some of the things the actors are seeing (point-of-view or POV shots) make the scene move visually.

Try listening to radio news and then immediately turn on the television and watch the news. Notice that the radio announcer speaks much faster than the television newsperson. Radio, like stage, is an auditory medium. If the radio newscaster pauses too long, we have what is known in the radio world as "dead air." The entire radio program comes to a screeching halt and then begins to drag from that point on. So the radio newscaster is setting the pace of the broadcast.

However, since television news is a visual medium, you not only see the news anchor in person, but you may also have footage to accompany the story. If the anchorperson pauses, so what? You still have her facial expressions to view. Again, the scene is carried visually.

Pauses, as mentioned in the section on human qualities, make it appear as though you are collecting your thoughts, but they also give the audience time to digest theirs and yours. This is definitely not to say that you should putt-putt along. You don't want the commercial message to drag.

Usually, something drags when there are gaps in the reading. There is a distinct difference between a gap and a pause. A gap is a break in the character, meaning that the actor has stopped the thinking and feeling process for some reason other than the right one. When someone pauses in natural conversation, he is still thinking and feeling what he is saying.

Over time, you'll get the idea of how fast or slow a particular script should be delivered. It all gets back to observation. Watch commercials to get an idea how quickly or slowly the actors in them say the dialogue. But the bottom line is, normally you should deliver the dialogue at about the same speed as you really would if you were just talking to someone in real life in that particular situation.

To repeat, not only should you observe commercials, but you should also observe people in real, everyday conversations. Interestingly, most people in real life pace things pretty well. There is a natural ability in real life to have an irregular pace. In fact, in real life you would have to work very hard to have the exact same pacing throughout a conversation. It is very unnatural, and again, an actor has to work very hard to be unnatural.

Accents and Dialects

I know people make fun of Arnold Schwarzenegger and Sylvester Stallone. But keep in mind that they have done a lot for actors. Before them, good speech was a requirement for an actor.

Obviously, I'm jesting, but accents and dialects are sometimes used in commercials. Let's start with the basics. Do you know the difference between an accent and a dialect? Most people don't. Most actors use the two terms interchangeably, but in reality they mean different things. If someone comes from the southern part of the United States, does he have a southern accent or a southern dialect? Most people would say "accent," and most people would be incorrect.

For people who live in the United States, there is no such thing as a southern accent. By definition, "accent" is foreign and "dialect" is regional. People who come from the southern part of the United States have a southern dialect. Similarly, people who come from Boston have a Bostonian dialect. However, if someone comes to the United States who was born in Italy, for example, he would have an Italian accent. If he came from Spain, then he would have a Spanish accent. Here's a test question: what if someone has a cockney—is that an accent or a dialect? Think about this one. It really depends on where the person is. If he were in England, cockney would be a dialect, since it would be regional. If he were in the United States, it would be an accent, since it would be foreign.

Now that we're clear on the difference between the two, should you use an accent or dialect when performing in a commercial audition? If the script doesn't call for it, the short answer is no. If the director had wanted an accent or a dialect he would have put it into the script or informed you in person at the audition.

I guess there are always exceptions to everything, but this would really be an "exceptional" exception, especially in a commercial audition. It might be more appropriate to try an accent or a dialect when it is not called for in a television or feature film audition than in a commercial audition, since advertisers are usually less open about what they want in a character than are television and feature film directors.

What about putting an accent or dialect in if it's called for in the script? The short answer is yes. There's a reason it's in there. Here's where it gets tricky: what if you can't do the accent or dialect required? Is it better to fake it and try to get away with it, or is it preferable to just show them you can act and not ruin your performance by such a bad imitation of an accent or a dialect? You'd have to choose between faking it and not following directions. It's not a great choice. It's sort of like when the doctor asks, "Ointment or suppositories?"

It really depends on just how bad your rendition of that accent or dialect is. If it's in the script, then it has been decided by dozens of people that this is what is called for. So normally you should give it your best shot. I guess there are those few occasions, and I mean few, where it might be better to first show them you can act and pray they'll love you so much that they'll be willing to work with you on the accent or dialect.

However, it might be better not to go on that audition in the first place. The last thing you want to do in an audition is ruin your reputation with those people for future castings, simply because you look so pathetic trying an accent or dialect that doesn't work.

Keep in mind that when it comes to national commercials, especially, we're not dealing with the high school play. In high school or college, the director is pretty much limited to students in the school or surrounding community. However, in a national or regional commercial, we have the resources to find good actors who have natural accents or dialects from whichever country or region we need.

Cue Cards versus Scripts

In the actual shooting of a commercial, very rarely would you be allowed to read from a script, and rarely would cue cards be used. By the time you arrive on a set, you usually have had some time to learn your lines. But during most commercial auditions, you will be permitted to peek at your lines either from a copy of the script or from cue cards.

For one thing, you will have had only a short time to look over the script. For another, the committee is usually in such a hurry when it comes to casting a commercial that there's no time to give you the script to take home and memorize. So, as far as the audition is concerned, don't worry if your photographic memory still has the lens cap on.

If you are auditioning for a commercial solo, you probably will be asked to deliver your lines to the camera. Therefore, your attention must be divided between the script and camera, or cue card and camera, depending on the particular audition. Naturally, the more you look into the camera (i.e., into the public's eyes), the more sincere you seem to be. This is why you should arrive at the audition early—so that you'll have a chance to become familiar with the script.

Speaking from the Script

For some reason, many commercial acting classes teach their students to hold the script way off to the actor's right or left. This way, according to the instructors who teach this nonsense, the script is out of the way, and the people viewing the playbacks won't notice it. *Huh?* First of all, most commercial auditions are in the form of a cold reading. We know you have a script in your hands—hence the term "cold reading." Secondly, who cares if you have a script in your hands? We certainly don't!

So, instead of putting the script way off to one side trying to hide it—which, ironically, it doesn't—why not hold it right in front of you, just below the lens? I'm talking about a single-person commercial where the actor is speaking directly into the camera. If you hold the script directly below the lens, your head won't be swinging way over to the right or left of the frame, and you can look at the script for a longer period of time.

If you hold the script right under the lens, we can still see that you are reading from a script because your eyes are glancing down slightly. However, it's a much smoother read because you'll have more time to look at the script and camera. With the script to your far right or left, your head is spending more time going from the script to the camera than if the script is just under the lens.

If you hold the script too high, you will cover your face—a no-no. The script should not be above your chin. Actors tend to think that because they can see over the script their faces are not hidden. Your eyes are much higher up on your face than your chin is, so the fact that you can see over the script does not necessarily mean your entire face is in view.

Also, if you hold the script too high, it may end up in the bottom of the frame lines. Is this a problem? Not really—unless it covers part of your face. There is nothing wrong with asking whether the script is in the frame lines; in fact, it is advisable. This is assuming they are shooting you in a close-up, since in a wider shot it will most likely be in the frame anyway. Recall from chapter 2 that you should always inquire as to where the frame lines are.

If you hold the script too low, you create a bobbing-for-apples effect. You have to hold your head down to read from the script. Then you have to bring your head back up to say a few lines. Then you have to bring it back down again to read from the script. Watching a bobbing head in a playback is about as annoying as being in the company of a sweaty sumo wrestler.

This bobbing-for-apples routine can make your face drop completely out of the bottom of the frame, where you might not be seen at all if you're being framed in a close-up. And even if it doesn't go that far, your face still might "fall" enough that the audience sees only the top of your head—not a pretty picture! Keep in mind that all or most of the people responsible for casting will be seeing you on the playback, not in person at the audition. So it's important for us to see as much of your face as possible during all or most of your audition.

If the dialogue in the script is written any farther down the page than the very top, fold the paper so that the dialogue is at the very top of the page. This way you can keep your head higher up. You don't want your face buried farther down the page than necessary. Also, if there is a lot of room at the bottom, you might want to fold that part up, so that the page becomes smaller. The smaller the page, the less paper there is to rattle if you're nervous.

Speaking from Cue Cards

In the smaller markets, you will rarely be furnished cue cards during auditions. In nonunion commercial auditions, the people auditioning you aren't required to provide them. However, in a union commercial audition it is required that we provide cue cards or a teleprompter for you. (Teleprompters are discussed later in this chapter.)

Most clients would rather not have to make cue cards available to you. It's much easier for them to just type the script onto paper than it is to write it out on cue cards. And if there are to be any changes, which is usually the case, they don't have to worry about making those changes on the cue cards. However, many actors actually like cue cards better. Whether cue cards are provided or not, you have the right to use a script if you'd rather. This is true whether the audition is for a union or a nonunion commercial.

With cue cards you don't have to worry about the bobbing head problem. On the other hand, sometimes people can tell that you are reading from them because they can see your eyes and head moving back and forth as you read from the left of the card to the right. That's fine. Again, as with a script, we know you're reading from a cue card. After all, we provided it!

One way to make this reading smoother and not make it look as though your eyes are shifting everywhere is to move your head slightly as you talk. I said *slightly!* If an actor's head is vertically stationary for a long time, you'll see his eyes moving across the cue card. Any head movement should be small, as though you are just gesturing with your head; I don't mean you should be swishing your head back and forth constantly. A slight head movement will compensate for your eye movements, making them much less noticeable. The idea is to try to read down the center of the cue card while catching the words with your peripheral vision, rather than reading across the lines.

When cue cards are provided, usually a script is available to the actors in the lobby when they arrive. It is absolutely imperative that when you arrive in the actual audition room, you look over the cue card at least once before you audition. First of all, cue cards are frequently handwritten. Often the person who wrote out the cue card isn't an intellectual giant; he's the type that had to take remedial sandpile and probably attended medical school to learn how to write.

Secondly, the line breaks are different from the script to the cue card. You're expecting lines to break at certain places since they were that way on the script, but now the line breaks are in strange places. Even individual words will probably be divided in places where they might not have been in the script. Believe it or not, this can really mess you up in an audition. You want to be utterly familiar with the cue card before just diving into the reading.

Thirdly, many times changes are made to the script. It's easy for the auditioners to retype a script. However, it's a much more daunting task to redo the cue card. I can tell you that nine times out of ten, when a script has been changed, the cue card will remain the same. And often the account executives, whose brains are engaged in unauthorized activities, phone us while we're in the middle of auditioning actors to let us know of changes that need to be made to the script.

If the placement of the cue card is not good for you, by all means, ask the auditioners to move it. Cue cards are placed according to the one-size-fits-all method. Some actors might be farsighted or nearsighted, and the cue card may be hard to read. Actors are generally hesitant to ask for the cue card to be moved out of some kind of fear of what the auditioners will think.

What is on the screen is more important than what took place to get it there. As I said earlier, the people who will be making the final decisions probably won't even be at the audition, especially if it's the first round of auditioning and not callbacks. (During callbacks it is very possible that the people making the final decisions will be present.) But, again, even if the bigwigs are there, it is better to have the cue card where you want it and give a good audition.

If you're using a cue card with another actor, usually the dialogue for each character will be written in different colors. This helps you to quickly spot which set of lines is yours.

The Teleprompter

You're probably familiar with the teleprompter. This device consists of a piece of glass angled right over the lens of the camera. Words are reflected onto that glass. Another person controls the speed of the text as it scrolls across the glass.

Teleprompters are rarely used by actors in actual commercial shoots. For one thing, commercial scripts are very short, and we figure that for what we're paying you, you could at least memorize a few lines. They are used routinely for infomercials, however, since the copy is usually longer. Also, infomercials sometimes contain very technical information utilizing words that may be hard to memorize and pronounce.

Teleprompters are used on almost all daytime serials. Way back when I was an actor on *General Hospital,* we relied very heavily on the teleprompter, since each episode consisted of a hundred or more typed pages. We did a play every single day! It would be extremely difficult to learn six hundred pages of dialogue or more per week.

The teleprompter is also used by newspeople. It makes it possible for the newscaster to seem to look right into the lens (i.e., into the eyes of the audience). Many times the newscasters have sheets of paper in front of them and turn one over every once in a while. Why do they do this? Interestingly, studies have shown that if someone stares into the lens for over thirty seconds or so, it can make some people in the viewing audience feel uncomfortable. When someone is talking to you and looks you right in the eye for an entire conversation, at some point you'll begin to feel uneasy. Also, when someone looks directly into the camera lens for too long, his eyes will appear to cross. For these reasons, many newscasters have a few sheets of paper in front of them so they can look at the sheets for a moment from time to time. Often there's nothing even written on them! But they give the newscaster a place to look instead of just staring into the lens the entire time.

Industrial and medical films and videos also make frequent use of the teleprompter. The scripts in these formats are usually longer than they are for commercials. As with infomercials, the dialogue can be technical, and many words may be hard to pronounce. We directors love to use the teleprompter with these types of shoots. We know that it makes you feel more comfortable and generally helps the shoot move along faster and more smoothly. The teleprompter also enables a writer to make changes quickly. With the cue card system, changes are hard to make. Either we have to cross out words and scribble new words in above the crossed-out ones, or someone has to redo the entire cue card. This is time-consuming.

Reading from a teleprompter isn't much different from reading off a cue card. As with cue cards, if the actor keeps his head perfectly still, then the eye movements across a line become very evident. Again, this doesn't mean your head should be bobbing along constantly. And as with cue cards, the actor should try to read down the middle of the text, catching the words on the left and right in his peripheral vision.

The Earprompter

The earprompter is another device used in the visual media to try to get information to the person speaking. Next time you watch a newscast, look behind the ear of the person speaking. You'll see a little coiled wire running around the newscaster's neck to the back of his head. This is the earprompter, and it makes it possible for someone to give information to the newscaster while she is talking. She can receive last-minute developments in a newscast, changes to a script, or cues to when commercials are about to begin or end, among other bits of information. Earprompters are also used by actors in trade shows and conventions and sometimes in industrial and medical films and videos.

Earprompters are not easy to master. I wouldn't suggest using one for an actual job until you have spent a lot of time with the device. Basically, a voice (usually the actor's own), which has been recorded on a cassette, is telling the user what to say. So the actor not only has to listen to the words, he has to repeat them as new words are being fed to him.

We don't use the earprompter in commercials because commercial scripts are so short. However, if you're an actor who does all sorts of gigs such as trade shows and the like, it might behoove you to own such a device.

Memorizing the Script

I strongly advise against memorizing the script in a commercial audition in the major markets. It's not a memory contest. I have never sat in an audition where a client turned to me and said, "Hey, he memorized it. Let's cast him." No one is impressed by the fact that you can memorize a few lines of copy in ten or so minutes. (There are a few exceptions to the above when you're dealing with some of the smaller markets. If you're in a small market, it's best to check with the local people to see whether they want you to memorize the script.)

Keep in mind that the audition is not the shoot. We're not necessarily looking for a polished performance at this point. We're basically looking for a good cold reading. Although this book doesn't deal with sitcom auditioning, people in that medium sometimes have a different take. Sitcom guest stars have very little time for character development. The directors and/or producers in this medium pretty much want to see something close to a performance, even in the audition.

Some actors think it is a good idea to memorize the script to show us that they're a quick study. But this isn't about being a quick study. We're going to take it for granted that you'd be able to memorize a few lines of dialogue by the time we actually shoot this ad.

When you spend your time in the lobby trying to memorize the script, you are taking valuable time away from what you should really be working on, which is how to make the script sound more human. That, and not your photographic memory, is what will impress us. Frankly, hardly any actors in an actual audition who think they have memorized the script ever get all the way through the audition without asking to view the script again. Your nerves start acting up once you walk into the audition room, and that clever delivery you had while working privately before the audition is now out the window.

One of the main reasons you shouldn't waste your time trying to memorize the script is the "staring factor." When you memorize something quickly, your eyes are actually looking back into your brain as you see the script in your mind. You could actually tell me every line break, every mark on the page, and so on, because you have "photographed" that page. That's what happens when you memorize something quickly. So we get this stare in your eyes. I can't tell you how many times in actual auditions a client has turned to me and said, "How come all these actors have that strange stare in their eyes?"

The next question the client will ask me is, "How come their eyes do that jerking thing?" Do you know what "that jerking thing" is?

Every few seconds the actor's eyes will move in a fast jerk. That's the actor's eyes actually ending on one line of copy in the script and going to the beginning of the next line. Remember that the actor is "seeing" the script in his mind.

But the main reason you shouldn't memorize the script in an audition is psychological. If you memorize the script, that's a *performance*. If you glance at the script or cue card every once in a while, even if you do have it memorized, that's a *cold reading*. Psychologically speaking, cold readings are going to get better, but performances are not. After an actor has left an audition, I've had clients say to me, "Wow, what a great cold reading, I can't wait to see his performance." In other words, we're giving you the benefit of the doubt because you don't know the script yet and we think it will get much better when you do have it memorized. If you already have it memorized when you audition, we don't think it will get much better by the time we actually shoot the commercial.

If you're one of those people who just have to have something memorized to feel more comfortable, fine. But it would be a smart idea to glance at the script or cue card a few times during your reading to at least give the impression that you're giving a cold reading. And in spite of everything I've just said, it is sometimes helpful to memorize the first and last lines, or at least the first few words of the first line and the last few words of the last line. That way you can start by looking at the camera or your partner, and you can end by looking at them, too. Don't make too big a deal out of this, but it is helpful.

The exception to memorizing the script would be in the case of young children. If a child doesn't read, then obviously it would be better for him to have it memorized. And if a child is a poor reader, then the more familiar he is with the script, the better off he'll be in the actual audition.

In a union commercial it is against regulations for us to ask you to memorize dialogue without providing you with compensation. If you are asked to memorize a commercial script in a union audition, you are to be paid one-half of a regular session fee. A session fee is the amount of money you are paid for the original shooting of a commercial. In 2005, a day's pay for a commercial shoot is a minimum of $535.00, so you should be paid $267.50 if you're asked to memorize dialogue in an audition.

Be careful about changing dialogue in an actual audition. If you can't find your place and add a word to help you get back to the script, no one's going to penalize you. But paraphrasing is a whole different ball game. Even adding such words as "You know," "Well," or "Yeah" can change the entire meaning of a script.

In *How to Act and Eat at the Same Time: The Sequel,* I have an entire chapter devoted to not dissing people or the script. I've had actors come into a commercial audition and say, "Who wrote this %&@$"? Many times the writer of the %&@$ is sitting in the room. Maybe I wrote the %&@$. We don't want to hear about what %&@$$y writers we are. Many times we think the script is %&@$$y too, but we don't need you to tell us about it.

After the Dialogue

At the end of any reading, please don't say "scene." I realize that very few actors do this in commercial auditions, although I have seen it on a few occasions. It is more common in television and feature film auditions, although just as inadvisable. Actors are notorious for doing this at the end of an audition where they are performing a monologue. You might as well put a sign on your forehead that reads, "Amateur."

While many acting instructors teach you to do this at competitions and in acting classes, it is totally inappropriate in an actual screen audition. We should know that the scene is over by the way you end your performance. You shouldn't ever have to say, in effect, "I'm done. That's the end of my audition." *Show* us that it's the end of your audition, don't *tell* us.

Basic Commercial Acting Principles

5

*Actors get paid for the things they think and feel,
not for the things they say.*

This book is a practical guide, not a theory-oriented one. I will touch on a few ideas utilized in some of the popular acting methods that can be applied to acting in commercials, but if you're looking for heavy method-acting books, there are plenty on the bookstore shelves.

I'm sure those books have a lot to offer. Many instructors who teach acting are on a much higher (or lower) plane than I am. A lot of these teachers do a fantastic job and are a credit to their profession. However, the difference between God and some of these acting instructors is that God doesn't think he's an acting instructor. Since I'm too simple-minded to grasp the true meaning of many of the theories out there, we'll just touch on a few extremely basic concepts that actors commonly use.

There are as many theories of acting out there as there are acting instructors. You should study all their methods if you're going to be a television, feature film, commercial, and/or stage actor. Some of these theories will help you in commercial acting and some will not. But whatever you do, it is important to keep studying your craft, for it is impossible to travel in the wrong direction and reach the right destination. Continuing to study your craft is like riding a bicycle: if you don't keep pedaling, you'll fall. Studying acting is a college from which you never graduate.

No More Drunken Polar Bears

When I was in high school, back when I was young enough to know everything, I was a real smart-aleck. My parents were very supportive of my acting ambitions, and in the summer of my sophomore year of college they sent me to New York City to study acting. I can't recall the name of the prolific supposed guru with whom I was going to study, but he had some sort of a German-Russian accent (I know that makes no sense) and a beard, so we thought this guy was the Second Coming. I'm sure he invented the accent himself. He also had traveled all the way from Russia, so we figured he had to be an expert. You know, an expert is just an ordinary guy who is at least a hundred miles from his hometown and carries a briefcase.

So we all eagerly arrived to meet the great and wonderful Oz. We figured $500 for a one-day session was a small token for the privilege of meeting this magnificent legend, because we realized that the only thing more expensive than education is ignorance. Keep in mind that $500 in the 1970s would be the equivalent of several times that amount today. There were about thirty of us in the room, so financially he did pretty well that day.

The guru was announced by his friend as he entered the room. He was dressed somewhat like Bart Simpson and reminded me of the type of guy who mops up at X-rated movie theaters. If the body is a temple, his was an amusement park. His toupée looked like ear-to-ear carpeting. (Although I was young, I was old enough to realize that toupées only fool people who wear them.) He was somewhere between ninety and death—so old his blood type had been discontinued. We thought he had a bad complexion, but we found out later that they were harpoon scars. The last time I'd seen something that looked like him, I flushed it.

He spoke for an hour about his "thriving career." (The great thing about an egotist is that you don't have to worry about him going around talking about other people.) Then he stuck his arm straight out in front of him, dividing the room with his outstretched fingers, waved his hand from the middle of the room to the left, and said, "From here ova, ve all going to be twees."

He stuck his hands in the air as if they were branches and swayed back and forth, instructing us to do the same. Half of the group followed suit—fifteen people acting like trees. It was starting to look like some strange exercise class. The actors swaying back and forth didn't resemble a forest; they just looked like they were doing the wave.

Then the guru stuck his hand straight out as before, fingers all pointing forward as he divided the room again. He swung his hand from the center of the room all the way over to the right and said, "And from here ova, ve all going to ve vind. Ve vind."

To demonstrate, he put his left hand against his left cheek and his right hand against his right cheek as he blew air from his mouth and moved his hands forward to demonstrate that the wind was moving forward. So fifteen people started blowing air.

"Vind blow, twees sway."

It was an awful sight. Here you had fifteen people on one side of the room blowing air toward the other side with their hands moving out from their cheeks, while the other fifteen people on the other side of the room had their hands straight up in the air while their bodies swayed back and forth. You would have sworn it was a rock concert in the 1960s where everyone was on some kind of heavy medication.

After about five minutes of blowing and swaying (I was a blower), I stood up in front of the entire class and said to him, "Sir, what *might* be the purpose of this?"

He stared me down and remarked, "Vhat, vu troublemayka? It's to learn how to veact, to veact."

Okay, I guess this "troublemaker" didn't know how to "react" to another actor, so I continued blowing while others continued swaying.

A few minutes later he said, "Now ve all going to ve drunken polar bear."

As a smart-aleck kid, I just couldn't resist this one. I walked up to the front of the class and asked the other students, "How many here have seen a drunken polar bear, and how often does the part come up?"

He told me to go to the back of the room and sit down. I took that as a reprimand. The next thing he said was, "Inside of every man eez part voman, and inside of every voman eez part man." I couldn't take it any longer.

I stood up and said, "Well, the woman inside this man must be a lesbian because she likes women."

"You, troublemayka, out," he demanded.

I was ejected from the class as he gave me the same look I got from Plaintiff during my divorce proceedings. I was actually glad to be thrown out of the class. It was as much fun as watching the Wicked Witch of the West dissolve. I learned two big lessons that day: (1) that I was a smart-ass, and (2) that all gurus aren't created equal. I didn't mean to be disrespectful, but I just couldn't see the learning curve of my acting going upward by my becoming a drunken polar bear.

I don't want to put down any type of acting method, because it is a good idea to study every method out there. Then you can choose which methods, or which parts of certain methods, work for you. But if a method doesn't work for you, it doesn't mean you're not a "real actor," as many instructors love to tell their students.

The Banging-Your-Head-against-the-Wall Method

In the late 1980s, when I was writing and directing my first film at Universal Studios, I got a real shock from one of the lead actors in the film. He phoned my office at Universal a few days before principal photography was to begin and said it was vital that we meet before filming got underway. He arrived at the studio the next day. He informed me that it would be extremely important for me to give him at least a two-minute warning before I was ready to use him for each new scene. I told him that wouldn't be a problem since I would always know a few minutes beforehand when he would be called to the set for each new series of shots.

Curiosity was getting the better of me, so I asked him why this notice was so crucial. He said that his acting method was a little off-beat, but that it was essential to his success as a star. He said he beats his head against the wall of his dressing room for two minutes before each scene. His reasoning was that it was like meditation and would help him think about the character. Maybe, but I was wondering how many acting jobs he was going to get in the future if one day he was down to twelve brain cells. It was becoming apparent to me that his gene pool needed a bucket of chlorine.

At the end of the first day of shooting, the two actresses whose dressing rooms were on either side of the actor's came to me in a rage. One of them said, "We don't know what is going on in the dressing room between us, but whatever it is, it has to stop because it's knocking our mirrors off the walls." Actually, that's not a direct quote, since I can't print her actual language suffice it to say that I think she had Tourette's syndrome.

The actor wasn't kidding when he said he needed to bang his brains out. But the bottom line is, he's a great actor and did a great job in that film. Directors don't really care what method you use. What we care about is that you give a true and believable performance. Whatever it takes to get you there is your business. My college degrees are in theater, and I can remember spending many hours doing mirror exercises and trust exercises and crawling around on the floor acting like a lion. I'm not putting any of these exercises down. I admit that I don't really understand them, but better minds than mine do.

So the information below is not technical acting information, and it's not anything out of the ordinary. It's just some basic thoughts about acting that you can take or leave. If you're in a serious acting class, these ideas might be elementary, but you can probably still think of them as a reminder to keep things simple, especially when dealing with acting in commercials. On the other hand, if you're just getting started as a commercial actor, what I'm going to tell you in this chapter might be very helpful.

The general public has the idea that acting in commercials isn't really an acting job. This couldn't be further from the truth. Commercial acting is one of the toughest acting jobs you could ever have. In a commercial you must take a few hours', days', or weeks' time and compress them into a believable sixty seconds or less.

There is no time for character development during this short period of time. The lines you might have to deliver probably won't be everyday real-life dialogue. You won't have complete freedom to choose your rhythm, because the commercial will have to be delivered in a specific amount of time. And you must create a likable character with whom the public can identify.

When you see a commercial on television, you might think to yourself, "Well, they just picked that person off the street. Anyone can do that." Or maybe you see another one and think, "Hey, I can be that obnoxious (or earnest, or thrilled, or snobbish), too." But can you create that impression without any artistic and technical training?

The public may assume that the people in those consumer interview ads, for example, are just cornered by an interviewer at the local shopping mall, that their responses are off-the-cuff, and that they've never been on television before. In actuality, they are probably very experienced actors speaking from a prepared script. Rarely is a person simply picked off the street and put into a commercial. The actor playing the part is giving you that illusion. That's a credit to his performance. Folks, commercial acting ain't easy, but it's not as difficult as many instructors make it out to be.

Stage, television, and feature film actors might find commercials much more difficult than they imagined. There are a number of restraints on the actors in commercials—time, unconventional dialogue, selling a product instead of a character, and so on. Acting in commercials requires some very basic acting principles, which are outlined below.

Frame of Reference

I hear actors say they "become" the character they're portraying. Hogwash! You can't "become" another person. No matter how hard you try, you're still going to react in certain ways that are personal to you regardless of the character you're portraying. Let's just face facts: there is no way you can have all the same exact feelings as another human being. The reason is that it's impossible for you to have the same frame of reference as another individual. You just haven't experienced the same life as anyone else. You're seeing the character through *your* eyes. And you will not interpret the character the same way as another actor would. If everyone had the same frame of reference, then everyone who played Hamlet, for example, would play the character exactly the same. But each of us sees Hamlet from our own perspective, so each person will play the character differently.

For another example, let's take a character who's going through a divorce. You're playing this character, who at one point says the line, "This is going to be a messy divorce." Everyone will reflect on that line differently, depending on his or her own experiences with divorce. You might read it one way if you are personally going through a messy divorce, differently if you are going through a friendly one, another way if you've never been married, and still another if you yourself are happily married. You would probably say the line yet another way depending on whether your parents are divorced or not. These are only a few of the thousands of variables that will influence how you'll deliver that line.

There is actually no way you can remove what's personal about your own interpretation, and, really, no one should want to. That's what makes your portrayal of a character unique and different from that of the other actors who will be auditioning for the same role. This is not to say that one interpretation is better or worse than the next. It is only to say that they are different. It is true, of course, that some interpretations might be more interesting than others. These variations are what give your characters "character."

So how might you give a successful interpretation of a role for which your personal experiences have not prepared you? You can expand your frame of reference beyond your own experiences. You learn to do this through observation, which is one of the greatest continuing studies you can do for your acting career, whether it be in commercials, stage, television, and/or feature films.

Observation

Let's say one day your agent sends you to an audition for the part of a doctor. Although you might have played doctor with a member of the opposite sex in the third grade, you don't really know the tensions, the worries, the decisions, and the condominium problems with which a doctor must contend. You are in a panic over how to portray a character you don't really understand.

The next day, your agent sends you to an audition for the part of an Arctic explorer. You are still trying to recover from the day before, when you had to recall your third-grade experience to portray that doctor. What diverse characters! The screen test takes place on a sound stage at Universal Studios, where it's so hot under the lights that when you get up from a chair, it follows you. But you must act cold just the same. Do you know how to act cold? Do you know how people look, feel, and react under such circumstances? Do you even know how *you* react to hot and cold temperatures? Perhaps you don't.

As an actor you're going to play all kinds of roles. You might not have the time to study a particular character before shooting a commercial, and you might not have any time to even think about the character before an audition. In fact, you might not even know what type of character you're going to audition for before you actually get there. This is the rule rather than the exception in commercial acting. So you must be prepared to audition as a variety of characters.

There is no way to learn everything about all types of people and professions, but one tool that will help you to understand people, to improve your interpretation, is observation. Commercial actors are usually placed in environments that are typical for the average person. They may not speak dialogue that is typical, but the occupations and situations are usually fairly normal.

Most actors realize the importance of watching other actors perform. This is very important, but many actors tend to forget that actors are interpreting roles (i.e., real people). So watch actors' performances, but also get to the source—watch people in real-life situations.

Next time you are in a doctor's office, for instance, observe the patients in the waiting room. Observe who seems anxious and/or nervous. Look around to see who is expecting news—good or bad. When you get into the doctor's office, watch the way the doctor acts, reacts, studies, and feels. Watch the precision with which he makes his diagnosis. Notice the way he takes down your history. Really listen to what he says and really pay attention to his facial reactions and expressions.

Now this doesn't mean that the next time you read for the part of a doctor, you should just follow in the footsteps of the one doctor you observed. You should observe many doctors and end up with observations that you can use for the future. Most characters you play will be a composite of your observations. You will find that some people in the same profession share some characteristics. (For instance, all doctors write your prescriptions illegibly and your bills clearly.)

When you have to audition for the part of a *particular* doctor, you can draw upon the traits from the doctors you have observed that fit that particular character. Since all actors will be drawing from different examples, all the actors who are auditioning will portray that doctor differently.

The same applies to the role of an Arctic explorer. Even if you haven't been to the Arctic lately, you can still observe the way people react when they are cold. And even if you live in a warm climate, you can still watch "cold" reactions. Television news, television entertainment, commercials, magazine photos, and so on are among the many different ways to observe people in different situations. You can watch what they do with their hands, legs, and faces when they are cold. For instance, they may wrap their arms around their bodies, rub their hands together, shiver, and shift about restlessly.

You know that people do all of these things because you have observed them. And—very important—you probably have noticed yourself doing these very same things. Of course, all people in cold weather do not react the same way, but you might find some commonalties in their reactions. You can store these, as well as some of the uncommon reactions to cold weather you have observed, in your memory bank for future reference.

Observe everyday people in terms of their emotional types. For example, shy people and outgoing people do not have the same mannerisms. They walk differently, speak differently, sit differently, and even eat differently. Their expressions of such emotions as happiness, sadness, anger, and fear will be varied. And don't forget to make note of cultural and regional disparities. A New Yorker may show pride, embarrassment, anger, or surprise in a different way than a Texan, for example.

Not only should actors observe all these things, but we directors do the same thing. I am constantly drawing on my observations to give me ideas about particular scenes. For example, let's say I have to have a humorous scene in which a person drives up to a teller window at a bank. As the camera pans across the teller window area, I might put Braille on the keypad on the driver's side. Why do they put Braille on the *driver's* side?

Another example might consist of an airport scene. It always amazes me that if someone is standing in a long line at an airport and needs to go to the restroom, he'll ask some perfect stranger to watch his bags so that some *other* perfect stranger won't come steal them. That observation of how people react at airports could come in handy if I were directing, for example, a humorous scene in an airport with people standing in a long line.

I've noticed many convenience stores have a sign out front that reads, "No dogs allowed except seeing-eye dogs." I've always wondered: who's going to explain it to whom? The person can't see, the dog can't read—what's the point? But if I had a scene in which a person was walking into a convenience store, I might put that sign in the window.

Why do they put "Wanted" posters in the post office? What do they want me to do, write the guy? And how come they didn't hold the sucker when they took his picture? Why isn't "phonetic" spelled the way it sounds? I think you're getting the point.

I could go on and on and on about how important observation is to a director. But in an audition you're pretty much going to direct yourself. We give very little, if any, real direction in an audition. This is your time to show us what you can "bring to the table." Therefore, not only can observation help you in the actual shoot, but it can also be extremely useful in the audition process.

Research through Observation

You will want to observe commercials in order to familiarize yourself with the various approaches utilized by different companies. As far as physical type is concerned, it is a grave misconception that only beautiful people have a chance at commercial acting. In fact, this couldn't be further from the truth. In general, the "look" that sponsors want will depend upon both the product they are selling and the image they are trying to project. A company that sells beer, for example, might want an actor who appears tough and rugged, while one that produces wine might prefer someone who looks more refined and sophisticated. Similarly, a person who retains not water but pizza and Twinkies and who wears Orson Welles designer jeans might not be welcome in an ad for Diet Pepsi. If it's not apparent whether you have braces or your teeth are in prison, you might not be cast in a toothpaste commercial.

Also observe the clothes that actors you see in commercials are wearing. Keep in mind here, as before, the overall image and tone of the commercials you watch. In a cologne ad, for example, an actor in a sweat suit might find it difficult to relay sophistication to this audience. By the same token, women in evening gowns are rarely, if ever, seen in the faster-paced, family-oriented fast-food commercials. Humor, of course, is much more flexible. Anyone from women in tennis dresses to men in tuxedos can be funny.

You can even do research and observation by sitting on your duff in your living room. Let's say you're about to audition for a commercial for a particular bank. I'll bet that bank has a Web site. Visit the Web site and you can gather all kinds of information about that bank for your audition. Are there photos of people on the bank's Web site? If so, how are they dressed? What color clothes are they wearing? What physical types are they? You're directly viewing the image the company wants to portray. However, this absolutely doesn't mean you have to conform to these images in any way, shape, or form. You may be auditioning for a part totally opposite what you see on the company's Web site. However, the Web is just one more tool for observation.

You could also visit one of the branches of that bank. Look at the posters of the people hanging around in the lobby. Pick up some of the bank's brochures and look at the people in them. Observe the colors the brochures utilize. Again, this doesn't mean that you have to walk into their audition wearing clothes that match the colors of the models' clothes. It's just another observation tool.

If you're auditioning for a product found in stores, you could visit a store that sells that product and do some observing. For instance, if you were to audition for a Tide commercial, how about actually observing a box of Tide for the kinds of things I've just mentioned?

All the types of observation discussed here, and many others, can help you in your approach to commercial auditions. Then, when you audition for, let's say, a suntan lotion commercial, you will have a better idea of what physical and emotional type of person might be needed and how he should be dressed, and you'll be able to ascertain a general idea of what kind of overall image he should present. So start preparing yourself for the commercial acting profession right this minute. Start observing!

Character Objective

An adage in acting is that every character has an objective. Every character has a purpose and is searching for something or some outcome. This is also true in commercial acting. One of the first things you want to look for while preparing for an audition—or for an actual shoot, for that matter—is what your character's objectives are. Characters have a purpose.

Take the following commercial script:

BILL: You know, Susie, I could sure use a Cola-Cola right now.

SUSIE: Cola-Cola is the greatest. Nothing tastes like Cola-Cola.

BILL: So, would you like to join me? Let's go to Jimmy's Restaurant and have a Cola-Cola.

SUSIE: You're on.

In this mock ad, what are Bill's objectives? One is that he wants to be with Susie, to get to know Susie better with the future intent of perhaps having a date with her. The other objective is to satisfy his thirst. And, of course, Cola-Cola is the way to do that. So the character wants (1) to get to know Susie better and (2) to satisfy his thirst.

It's very important that you look for the objective(s) of the character. The objectives are always there to see, though sometimes they are hidden and hard to find. Find a purpose for your character and a reason for his actions. It will give your character more strength and provide a guideline for you when interpreting dialogue.

Memory Substitution

Suppose you get an acting role in which you have to yell at some person in this particular scene. This person has been treating you very badly (in the script) for the past six months and you have to give her a piece of your mind. And let's suppose you're a male and you're cast in the above scene. You must yell at this woman who is playing opposite you. So you arrive on the set early to meet your partner. But then, after talking with her for a few minutes, you find yourself thinking she's so beautiful she could make a stone pass out. She has curves in places where other women don't even have places and her figure reminds you of the Grand Tetons. Perhaps you're trying to decide whether she looks more like Ginger or Mary Ann. You really don't feel like yelling at her, but that's what the scene calls for.

Or let's say you are a female cast in a romantic role and you don't personally like the male the director has cast to play your boyfriend. He's not your type. In real life you have a Ph.D. in quantum physics, while he's the type who takes the phone off the hook to watch a *Baywatch* rerun. He's had his face lifted so many times that it's out of focus. Perhaps you've seen better-looking heads in a cabbage patch.

The point is clear: actors often have to be in situations that don't conform to their personal lives (or likes). As a matter of fact, because scenes are shot out of sequence (to be discussed in chapter 13), you might be in situations that are emotional opposites of each other during the same day, or even during the same hour, for that matter. One minute you might be shooting a scene in which you're supposed to be very happy, and a few minutes later you're shooting one in which you're supposed to be very sad, and so on. If you aren't convincing in each scene, then the entire show falls flat.

Many actors use something called *substitution*. We substitute for the current situation something called up from our memory. Let's take the first example above—the male who has to yell at a woman in one particular scene. You have never met this person, yet you have to tell her how horribly she's been treating you for the past six months.

Remember that in real life, when you look at her, you melt. She's as exciting to you as finding an old friend who works at Dreamworks. You must substitute something in your mind for the situation at hand. Perhaps you could concentrate on a woman whom you personally dislike and carry those feelings over to the person you're playing opposite. Maybe you'd like to wrap a pound of hamburger meat around that woman's neck and make her play with the neighbor's German shepherd. The anger, meanness, and hatred will come through.

As for the second example, let's suppose you're the female lead and you have to tell your male co-star how much you love him, and then, on camera, for millions of people to see, give him a kiss so long it would cost fifty dollars in a taxi. You're supposed to be in love with him, but in real life he's the type that quotes Howard Stern. Again, you can substitute with the feelings you have for someone you really do love at that particular time in real life. It all sounds easy enough, but it takes a lot of concentration to pull it off. The actor has to accept it first, and then the audience will follow suit.

Suppose you have to play a murderer in a particular film. What if you've never murdered anyone? Perhaps you've wanted to! Let's assume, for the sake of argument, that you're not in a federal penitentiary for homicide. Have you ever been so outraged that you had a hard time keeping your self-control? You could think back to that experience and use that rage when playing this murderer. Again, you're substituting one circumstance for another.

Let's take an example more specifically related to commercials. Suppose you're acting in a fast-food commercial in which you must take a bite out of a hamburger. We could easily do a hundred or more takes in a single day, meaning you would have to take bites from hundreds of hamburgers. Now, even assuming you really love hamburgers, at some point you're going to lose your enthusiasm for those burgers.

Obviously not many people can take a bite out of that many hamburgers. We actually have a "spit bowl" when shooting food commercials. A "spit bowl" is just that—a bowl to spit the food into when the camera stops rolling. Yeah, you're right—it's pretty disgusting. So perhaps you could imagine that hamburger being different types of food that you really do like and can convince yourself that you're eating a different food. Have you ever kissed someone and imagined that person being someone else? (Never mind—I don't want to go down that road!)

This technique has some critics, who say that an actor should not have to substitute for anything—an actor should be on his toes enough to "grab the moment" and be able to relate to the scene no matter what takes place in it. If an actor can do that every time, more power to him. But there are going to be scenes where you can't directly relate. And there are going to be times when the props you'll use are nothing like the real thing. Substitution may be necessary to get you through it all.

For commercial acting, be careful not to take all this to the extreme. I'm not saying you should take classes where you crawl around on the floor and act like a pig. If that type of acting exercise works for you, great. But these ideas concerning substitution are pretty standard and seem to work very well for most actors.

Backstory/Prelife

Many directors use the term "backstory" to designate what took place before the story began. In the case of a feature film, all the characters, unless they haven't been born yet, had a life before the film, known in acting circles as the character's *prelife*. Many times in a feature film script, the *backstory* is not hard to design. Frequently the script itself gives some information about what took place before the script begins.

We think of a feature film as a slice of life: something happened before the film, there's the film, and then life goes on after the film is over. Many times commercial lives also have a backstory. In other words, the people in these commercials had a life before the commercial begins in the script, their lives are in the story contained in the script, and their lives go on after the script has ended. So the story in the script is actually only a slice of life.

Suppose you are playing a character who is twenty years of age when a particular film begins. That character, obviously, has lived for twenty years, about which we have some information. There is a reason this twenty-year-old character acts a certain way at the beginning of the film, a reason that didn't just surface when he was twenty. So it is incumbent upon the actor to design a life that took place before the script began. This will give the actor an understanding of why his character acts in a certain way.

The same applies to a character in a commercial. Your character has a backstory. Even if you're just playing yourself, *you* have a backstory! This type of analysis must be done very quickly and efficiently in an audition. There's just not much time for lengthy character analysis, nor is it necessary. It is necessary, however, to have an understanding of why the character acts the way he does.

It really doesn't even matter if your backstory is way off base. In fact, I doubt the copywriters for the commercial did any backstory on the character. They might have given a lot of thought to the type of person this character should be, but it is unlikely they are going to give you much backstory about your character. It will be almost entirely up to you.

The Hero 6

*We're not doing Shakespeare;
we're selling French fries, for goodness' sake.*

*A*ny role you obtain in a commercial is really a supporting role. The most important role in any commercial is the product, not the actor. Advertisers want you to sell yourself only insofar as it enhances the selling of their product. The product is *numero uno.*

The product is taken very seriously on a set. We even hire special people whose jobs are to work solely not with the actors or the production, but with the product. For example, in a fast-food commercial we hire food stylists, people whose entire job is to make the product look its best. The food stylists actually have special tools to "dress" the food in its best light. If we were utilizing a hamburger in a fast-food commercial, for example, the food stylists would use special tools to move the sesame seeds around, to cut the lettuce just right—we might even put a thin coat of wax on the buns to make them shine.

Food stylists are a very important part of my team, and I am very careful when hiring these specialists. When the stylists have worked their expertise on several hamburgers, for example, the director will then view all of the "contestants." For each shot, one new hamburger among those will be chosen. That particular hamburger is known as the "hero." Usually, the "loser" hamburgers are either eaten by someone, saved for the homeless, or simply worked on to improve their look for future possible shots.

Since the hero is so important, it deserves its own special chapter in this book. Of course, you'll want to be sure you understand the terms and techniques in the preceding chapters. Then you can more effectively focus your attention and energies on the different aspects of dealing with the product, or "hero," explained in this chapter.

Mentioning the Product Name

You would think that this goes without saying: know how to say the name of the product. But believe it or not, many actors mispronounce the product name during auditions. This wouldn't necessarily keep someone from being cast, but it sure doesn't help. You need everything going for you in an audition. Often you'll be auditioning for a product you've never seen or whose name you've never heard because it hasn't been introduced to the public yet.

If you have any doubt as to how to pronounce the product name, ask! It's better to ask in the lobby, before you enter the actual audition room. The best person to ask is the casting director. That person will definitely know the correct pronunciation. Keep in mind that the casting director is on your side. She is part of your team. However, if for some reason you can't get an answer before you go into the actual audition room, then by all means, ask when you get in there. Remember, the bottom line is what's on the audition tape.

One of the most important things to do when auditioning for a commercial role is to make the product name stand out more than the rest of the script. This is the whole point of the commercial! After viewing a particular commercial, the audience should walk away from it at least remembering the name of the product. There are several ways to accomplish this, which I'll discuss later.

One word of caution here: the guidelines below are just that—guidelines. Please don't get so wrapped up in the suggestions below that your commercial begins to sound canned and/or rehearsed. As you audition, these suggestions should be in the back of your mind, not in the forefront. Keep in mind from the preceding chapters that the commercial must sound as though you are speaking naturally.

As mentioned earlier, one way to make any word stand out is to simply say the word a little louder than you do the rest of the words in the commercial script. Be careful, however, not to overdo this; you don't want to be obvious about it. Of course, the opposite is also true: the product name will also stand out if you say it a bit more softly. It's not necessarily whether the name is said louder or softer that makes it stand out, it's the difference in volume between the name of the product and the rest of the script that separates it from the rest of the text.

Don't take this suggestion too far. It would be better not to do it than to do it and be obvious about it. Brilliant actors can do it so subtly, you can't tell that that's what they're doing. And you remember the product name after they deliver the dialogue.

Another way to make the product name stand out is to treat it differently in tone and/or pace from the rest of the script, as described earlier. For example, you might be talking in a high-pitched tone of voice and then drop the pitch slightly when you mention the product name, returning to the higher pitch when reading the rest of the commercial. The reverse is also true. Or, if you're talking fairly rapidly while saying the dialogue, you could slow down slightly when you get to the product name. Again, you must do this very subtly, or you begin to look like the type that says "Hi, Mom" into the camera. (How come no one ever says "Hi, Dad"?)

Pausing, of course, is also a very effective tool. When a speaker wants to emphasize a certain point, he can pause right before he makes the point. This gives the audience time to gather the information already presented and to get ready for the next set of ideas. Try saying a sentence aloud and pausing before the most important word. You'll notice how that word stands out. Pausing right after the product name can have the same effect. Bottom line: *make the audience remember the product name.*

When you mention the name of the product in an audition, it helps if you look into the camera or at the actor with whom you're supposed to be talking (depending upon the setting of the commercial). This is not mandatory by any stretch of the imagination, so please don't spend too much time making sure you do it. However, it helps if you don't bury the product name while looking at the script or looking away at a cue card. Actually, it's better to say any line that mentions the product name directly to the camera or to your partner, depending upon to whom you're speaking. Again, this is only a thought, not an ironclad rule by any means. It may be difficult to use this hint in an audition when you are not very familiar with the script. However, with a lot of practice, you'll get better at it.

It usually makes good sense to smile when you mention the name of the product. It amazes me how many actors bury their heads in their scripts and frown while saying the product name. Again, this seems obvious to me, but based on what I constantly see in auditions, it apparently isn't obvious to most actors. I'm not saying you can forget being cast if you're not smiling and have your head stuck in the script when mentioning the product name. Most likely, no one thing about your performance would stop you from being cast. It's usually a combination of things that make a performance lackluster, and each item I've mentioned is but one piece of the puzzle.

I hesitated even to write down these suggestions about how to make the product name stand out, because I see many actors trying too hard to accomplish it. Then their performances become phony. It will take a lot of practice to make the product name stand out smoothly, so start working on it before you forcefully try these suggestions in actual auditions.

Words That Put the Product in Its Best Light

You should be aware of the words in the script that put the product in its best light. For instance, take the hypothetical commercial line, "Sparkle Toothpaste helps prevent cavities." The important words here are the product name and "prevents cavities." The word "helps" is utilized because advertisers must be certain that every statement made in a commercial is strictly true. Say the word "helps" clearly, but you probably wouldn't want to give it the same prominence you give to the words "prevents cavities." By doing this, you can make the commercial sound as though it is saying that Sparkle Toothpaste prevents cavities. You can't actually say that because it can't actually be proven, hence the word "helps."

Suppose we say that our product is "virtually trouble free." For you, the actor, "virtually" has less importance. By emphasizing the important words—"trouble free"—you make the product stand out and put it in its best light. And you make it appear as though the product is trouble free. Of course, we can't say that, hence the word "virtually."

If the script states that "XYZ has an effective ingredient that four out of five doctors recommend," what point is the advertiser trying to get across? Hopefully, the audience won't think it's that the product has one ingredient that four out of five doctors recommend. The ad agency wants to portray their product as being recommended by four out of five doctors. Of course, that's not what the commercial states, but it is the intent. The key words that don't need to stand out here are "effective ingredient."

Try this one: "acts like crystal." The product isn't made of crystal, or the script would have said that. However, the intention here is to make it sound as though it *is* crystal. So the important word is "crystal." You probably wouldn't want to emphasize the words "acts like."

Find the word that is key, from a legal standpoint, in this ad:

> The XYZ Roadster is America's number one mid-size selling car today.

If you picked "today," you'll get a negative buzzer on this game show. If you picked "mid-size," you can draw a vowel from Vanna because you are correct. "Mid-size" really narrows the field. If the word "mid-size" doesn't stand out, the audience might possibly walk away from that ad believing that the XYZ Roadster is America's number one–selling car. Of course, we can't actually say that, hence the word "mid-size."

I could give many more examples, but I think you get the message. Look over the script very carefully, searching for words that put the product in its best light, and make the product name stand out with those important words. Dozens of people, sometimes dozens upon dozens, have signed off on the script before it gets to you, the actor. We take every word very seriously, since they have all kinds of legal implications.

Start really *listening* to commercial dialogue when you view commercials on television and listen to them on the radio. You'll be amazed at how many of them are written with these types of insinuations. You'll begin to hear words you've never heard before because the actor delivered them in such a way as to not make those words stand out.

We work very hard on these scripts. Just imagine how much money is spent for each word of a commercial script, especially when you consider all the costs not only of producing the commercial, but of airing it over and over again on television. Each word costs a staggering amount of money.

Handling the Product

In an actual shoot, we'll tell you how we want you to hold the product. We're very picky about that, and we know exactly how we want it handled. However, in an audition you're on your own. We don't have the time or the patience to go into detail about how one should inter-act with the product. But how you relate to the product could have an impact on whether or not you are cast in a particular commercial.

Many times in actual shoots you won't even be the one handling the product in ECUs (extreme close-ups). (See chapter 13 for an expla-nation of the different types of shots.) In a big-budget commercial shoot, we'll usually hire a hand model. In this industry, some people refer to this person as someone who does "hand jobs." For obvious reasons, I prefer to use the term "hand model." These are people with nearly perfect hands who handle products in close-ups for a living. A hand model is an expert at hitting marks in thin air, marks that don't really exist. They know how to put that product in the exact place I want it almost every single time. They know how to "cheat" the product to the camera and how to angle it in a certain way so as to not reflect lights.

If you have great hands, a great behind, great legs, thighs, arms, ears, or anything else, you might want to consider being a *parts model*. The pay is almost the same as for the person speaking the lines—and you usually don't have to worry about product conflicts. We'll pay top dollar for a great pair of legs to be used for close-ups in, for example, a pantyhose commercial. Big money is made by parts models who just show their buttocks—for example, in a bathing suit commercial. For a jewelry commercial, a hand model is usually used for the ECU of the actual ring. A number of stars have parts models for close-ups of their body parts. Often, when you think you have seen a particu-lar star nude or partially nude in a feature film, you're really seeing someone else's parts. A star might even have three or four people on a film project who model different parts of his or her body.

When you shoot a commercial, especially for a major product, you generally have to sign an exclusivity contract. In other words, while your commercial is airing you can't perform in any commercial for a competing product. In fact, you can't be in a commercial for a competing product even if you're only being "held." (Being held means that your contract is still active, but the commercial, for one reason or another, isn't presently airing. However, you are still being paid, compensation known as a holding fee.) It would be very unusual for a parts model to be bound by an exclusivity contract if his face isn't shown. So this is a field in which you can continue to work even with products that compete in the marketplace. A close friend of mine is a leg model for about five of the very top female actresses. That would surely be a conflict in all other areas of this profession.

Again, in an audition you will almost always be doing your own handling of the product. Below are some basic ideas about how to handle the product that are pretty standard in the industry. However, these ideas should only be used for auditions, since the director will give you the exact information needed for the actual shoot. In smaller markets, you might be on your own even during the shoot, so the ideas discussed below will be helpful whether you're performing in a large market or a small one.

The commercial actor must be extremely careful not to conceal the label on which the name of the product is printed. When you hold the product, make sure not even one finger covers any part of the front of the package, especially the product name. You can hold the product from the back with your fingers on the sides, or you can hold the top of the product with one hand and the bottom part with the other. However you hold it, make sure that the product label directly faces the camera. Even holding the product just a little off to one side will usually cover part of the product name—a no-no!

Whether you are working alone or with another actor, it is usually best to hold the product close to or level with your face. Notice that in most commercials the actor will hold the product in this general area. Of course, there are thousands of exceptions. For example, in a Ford automobile commercial, you would find very few actors who are capable of holding an automobile next to their faces!

With small products, you don't want to hold the product too far below your face or way off to one side of it. The camera lens will naturally separate the product from you. (See chapter 8 for more information about camera separation.) If you hold the product off to one side of your face, the cameraperson will have to pull the camera back to get both you and the product in the shot. Therefore, your face will show up smaller. Your goal here is for the director (in the case of an audition) or the television audience (in the case of the actual airing) to see the association between you and the product.

The viewing audience will sense how you feel about a product just by the way you hold it. Hold the product as though you really like it. You've seen people holding things as though they couldn't care less about the object. Think nice things to yourself about the product; this will help you hold it with pride.

Miming and Props

Generally, miming a prop that isn't really there, unless you're asked to do so, can look awfully silly. So unless it is absolutely necessary, it's not a good idea to fake holding the product, or anything else for that matter. However, there are a few exceptions where it becomes necessary. If you have to talk on a phone and none is available, then it really looks awkward to just be talking into thin air while supposedly talking into the phone. This would be a case where you would probably want to hold your hands as though you are holding a phone. If it works for the particular script you happen to be performing, perhaps a better solution would be to pull out a cell phone. If you're going to use a cell phone, make sure you don't spend much time trying to get it open. Actors are often somewhat jittery in an audition, and fumbling with a cell phone only makes you appear more nervous and insecure. The best type to use would be one that is a complete unit, but the flip-opens can work fine in this situation if they open easily.

If you have to hold a coffee cup, for example, and one is provided for you in the audition room, then by all means use it. It would look strange for you to have your hands around a cup that isn't there. But the best thing is to try to stay away from miming any props unless it is absolutely necessary. For instance, when two people are supposedly sitting at a table talking, many actors for some unknown reason want to pantomime eating food and drinking something. This is so distracting that it calls more attention to itself than to either the product or your performance.

At some point your performance can become an audition about the prop and your miming of it, and not about the actor. Frankly, most actors mime props so poorly that their performances become phony. Many actors actually try to impress us with their miming abilities. We're not impressed. Hey, I personally love Marcel Marceau, but if we want a great mime we'll get him or some other great physical illusionist. And even if we were impressed, again, it would become an audition about miming and not about your acting abilities. Impress us with your personality and acting abilities. Everything else is secondary.

I know many commercial acting instructors tell their students to bring props to auditions. I strongly recommend that you not do this. When you bring in props other actors don't have, your audition turns into an audition about the props. Your props stand out more than your performance. If there is any question as to whether you should use a prop that you brought into an audition, err on the side of not using it.

Other exceptions, besides a phone, might include everyday things such as a wallet, pen, glasses, and so on. These types of everyday props won't stand out as much as a prop that isn't such a common item. Small, common props such as these do generally help the actor with his character. First of all, they can give the actor something to do, so that he isn't just standing there wondering what to do with his hands. Secondly, you work with small props every day. They are very familiar to you. So they will help you to do more natural things with your performance and to feel more comfortable.

One prop you might consider is a wedding ring. Whether you're married or not, a wedding ring is very appropriate for certain types of commercial auditions. For instance, if you're reading for the part of a married father in a commercial, psychologically you appear more like a married father if you're wearing a wedding ring; the same goes for a women reading for the part of a married woman. But you should be very cautious about using any other kind of jewelry.

Eating the Product

Handling food, when the food is the product itself, is another matter that most actors don't do very well. How you relate to the food before you eat it, when you eat it, and after you eat it is extremely important.

There are three basic steps to eating the product: the approach, the actual bite, and the reaction or revelation. Each director might have specific ways he wants the product tasted on his particular food commercial, but below are the basics. Keep in mind that during the audition you will get very little advice—in fact, probably none—about how to eat the product. So the suggestions below should help you a lot.

Let's begin with the approach phase. If the actor looks at the food and realizes he's going to love it, and then he eats it and does love it, then no revelation will have taken place. Let's suppose you're auditioning for a fast-food commercial in which you have to take a bite of a hamburger. You could begin by looking at the hamburger with skepticism—an attitude that says, "I'm not so sure this is really going to taste very good." Don't go very far with this. Too much skepticism would be too negative. It's just kind of a look of, "Well, let's see here, is this hamburger really as good as everyone says?"

The next phase is the taking of an actual bite. If the auditioners have any food present and you're supposed to take a bite, take as small a bite as possible. This is so you won't have a mouth full of food as you try to speak. Also, you don't want food flying out of your mouth as you're trying to deliver dialogue. For many obvious reasons, it would be extremely rare for the auditioners to actually have hamburgers present, for instance, for a fast-food commercial audition. Usually we'll have some type of food that is acceptable to just about everyone. A soda cracker is very common.

There are two traps that actors potentially fall into while taking a bite of the product: reacting to the food too quickly and reacting to it too slowly. If you react too quickly, it appears as though you're insincere. Next time you see a child trying out a new food for the first time, watch his reactions very closely. After the approach or skepticism phase, the child will take a bite, and his reaction will usually begin about two seconds later. It won't be immediate.

On the other hand, if you take too long to react, you're making two major mistakes: looking as though you really don't like it, and dragging out the commercial, using more air time than is warranted or needed. After you take a bite and have waited for the two-second reaction, your smile should grow quickly, though not all at once. Also, notice that after eating a bite of food, many actors in food commercials will take in a breath of air as their smile grows. So it appears, in a sense, as though they have been totally uplifted.

This reaction will be very powerful, since you weren't sure you were going to like the food at the outset. If you had thought you were going to like it and then liked it, no revelation would have taken place, and we wouldn't have convinced anyone of anything. If you're going to look like you've been totally convinced of the product's great taste after taking a bite, you need to look slightly skeptical at the beginning.

When tasting food, think of something you really like to eat. Does the word "substitution" come to mind? If you really like that particular food, then fine, no problem. But I can assure you that after you have had dozens of bites of it, it won't taste as good to you as it did before the shoot. It will begin to remind you of an astronaut's food package.

If you are really thinking of some food you actually like to eat, the emotion that will show across your face will come from within. And remember, emotions that come from within are generally much more honest and believable than ones that are technically manufactured from the outside. So it's better to play the action internally first, rather than just playing the reaction itself.

Why Most Multi-Person Auditions Don't Work

7

*In the great supermarket of life, may the wheels
on your grocery cart all move in the same direction.*

It's very important in a multi-person audition that all actors be doing the same scene. I don't just mean that they both have a script that has the same dialogue on each page. I mean that the actors are "on the same page" as far as the particulars in the script are concerned.

The best way to illustrate this is to use a true story. During a commercial audition I was holding at Universal Studios, these two actors (I'll refer to them as Jack and Jill) came in to read. They spent about fifteen minutes together in the lobby reading the scene together, as did all the other pairs of actors that were about to audition.

Jack and Jill arrived in the audition room as though they were ready to perform. After all, they had had plenty of time to prepare in the lobby and didn't spend that time talking with the other actors who were auditioning, as many actors do. I always ask the actors when they come into the actual audition room if they have had enough time to prepare. Both of them replied that they were as ready as they'd ever be.

They were both young and hormonal. Jack didn't seem quite as bright as Jill, although she wasn't exactly the type that could shout out the answers while watching *Jeopardy*. It was apparent from our ten-second conversation that to count to twenty-one he would have had to be naked. His family tree was probably a wreath. Let's be honest, I was afraid that someone would get hurt on the spikes in his hair. It was obvious that he was related to Don King.

Jill was in great shape and was the type that could have appeared in the *Sports Illustrated* swimsuit edition. I don't think she had silicone; I think she had helium. She had paid no attention to the shape of her lips when she put on her lipstick, and her clothes were so tight she must have had to jump off a roof to get into them. She had 1980s hair—big, permed, and yellow. Some of the guys in the office thought she looked great, but to me she looked like the Lion King.

Something seemed amiss from the very beginning of their reading. The scene was awful. It wasn't just bad; it was dreadful. However, individually they were terrific. Does that make any sense? They each did their respective parts very well, but together the scene was just not working. They just weren't *connecting* in any way whatsoever. Were their personalities so different that perhaps each one of them should have read it with someone else? Not by any stretch of the imagination.

Discussing the Scene in Advance

One of the main reasons most actors don't connect with one another in auditions is that very few actors discuss the scene together while in the lobby. They may read lines back and forth, but rarely do they take the extra few minutes to discuss the most important aspects of the scene.

I sent Jack out into the lobby for a few minutes while I asked Jill some questions about the scene. First I asked her, "What is the relationship, or is there one, between the two people in this scene?" She appeared to be irritated by the question. Her facial expressions went from a hummingbird to an enraged AK-47-packing kamikaze pilot.

Now, many of you might be thinking this is a dumb question—most actors would surely know the relationship of the people in the scene. You would be incorrect. Many times the actors just read lines back and forth and have no idea to whom they are speaking. Does it matter? You bet!

For instance, would you women play a scene the same if you were playing it as though the other actor was your cousin as opposed to your husband? You would play the scene differently depending on the relationship, right?

If one actor played the scene as though he and his female partner were married and the other actor played the scene as though they were dating, does that matter? *Absolutely*. You act differently when you're dating than when you're married. I think you see the point here. Two actors must be playing the same scene or there's just something about the scene that won't work.

Jill considered this question for a moment. Finally, she responded, "Well, brother and sister, I would suppose. It really doesn't say, but it seems as though we are related, or something of that nature. Yeah . . . it seems obvious that we're siblings. I mean, wouldn't you say?" At first she was pretty sure of her answer, but she seemed less so the more she thought about it.

The next question I asked Jill was, "How long have you been in this relationship?" Does it really matter? Do you play a scene differently depending on how long you've been in a particular relationship? *Absolutely!*

If one actor thinks you're on a first date and the other thinks you've been dating for five years, is that a different scene? Women, don't you act differently on the first date than on the twentieth? If one actor thinks you've been married for ten years and the other thinks you've been married for ten days, does that make a difference? (For an accurate answer, ask a married person.)

Jill was much surer of this answer, since it seemed so obvious to her. "Well, we're both about eighteen years old and since we're brother and sister, I'd say the characters have obviously known each other for about eighteen years. Yep, I couldn't be any more sure on this one."

I then asked Jill, "Where does the scene take place?" Does the location really matter? If you were on a date, would you act differently if you were dining in a Denny's restaurant as opposed to a high-class one? Think about it: the ambiance is different, the volume level of the room is different, the attitude of the people in the two places is different, and so on and so forth.

If you're female and you are on a date with a guy, would you play the scene differently if you were sitting on a couch in your living room with your parents in the next room than if you were in a van parked down by the river? The location totally changes how you play a scene. Teenage boys and girls talk differently if they are with their friends in a school locker room than if they are with those same friends riding in a car with one of their parents driving.

Jill's response was, "Well, since we are brother and sister, we're probably in our home."

Is "in our home" a complete answer? No, not really. You might play a scene differently in the kitchen, for example, than in the garage. So I pressed her a little further. "Where in the house?"

"Well, a common place that people in a house sit and talk is at the breakfast table. So, going by the dialogue in the script it seems pretty obvious that we are sitting at the breakfast table," she answered confidently.

My next question for Jill was, "What time of day or evening is it?"

Jill was getting tired of my questions. She seemed to be having about as much fun as you would watching a PBS pledge break. A few moments later she answered, "It's obviously early in the morning. I mean, since we are at the breakfast table having breakfast, it would just seem obvious to me that it would be in the morning."

Is "in the morning" a complete answer? Would you play a scene that was supposed to be taking place at six o'clock in the morning differently than one that was taking place at eleven o'clock in the morning? Your whole demeanor is different at these two different times. So the director in me was coming out as I pressed on.

"What time, specifically, would you say it was in this scene?"

"Oh, well, if we're having breakfast it has to be around seven o'clock in the morning."

You see, now Jill had built a scene. Instead of just reading lines, she had an understanding of the most important basics of that scene. Her scenario went like this: the two actors were brother and sister who had known each other for eighteen years, having a conversation while sitting at the breakfast table eating breakfast at seven o'clock in the morning. Jill was proud that she now knew more about the scene than she had when she walked into the audition room.

I called Jack back into the room. It was now his turn. I asked Jill to remain completely silent as I put to Jack the exact same questions, in the exact same order, with the exact same inflections in my voice.

"So, Jack, what is the relationship, or is there one, between the two people in this scene?" As he took a moment to think, Jack gave me a look reminiscent of Weird Al Yankovic. "Oh, well, we are obviously dating. It's pretty obvious that I have a crush on this girl as I'm just getting to know her."

Jill's mouth dropped wide open. She couldn't believe what she was hearing. I had to remind her to remain silent. She really wanted to disagree with Jack.

"And how long have you been in this relationship?" I asked Jack.

"It's apparent that we have just started dating. I think it's pretty safe to say that we haven't known each other very long."

What does "haven't known each other very long" mean? It means different things to different people. There's a great scene from Woody Allen's movie *Annie Hall*. Woody's character is in his psychiatrist's office on one side of the split screen, and Diane Keaton's character is in her psychiatrist's office on the other. Each psychiatrist asks, "Do you have sex often?" Woody's character answers, "Hardly ever—maybe three times a week." Diane's character answers, "Constantly—I'd say three times a week."

The point of the scene is that individuals look at things differently. So actors need to be very clear with each other about their scene. Be cooperative; when you help a person up the hill, you find yourself closer to the top. In the above scenario, a month of dating could be an eternity to one partner and a very short time to the other. So I continued to question Jack.

"What does 'very long' mean?"

A few moments later he answered, "Two weeks." I again could see Jill practically foaming at the mouth, wanting to disagree with him. I knew she wanted to have a discussion with Jack, but that discussion should have taken place long before this point. After I gave Jill a glance, she just smiled at Jack as I continued with the interrogation.

"So, where does the scene take place?"

He gave the typical male response: "In the bedroom." Jill's eyes really grew wide at this point, not with excitement but with astonishment.

"Whose bedroom?" I asked. Does it really matter? You might play the scene differently if you were in your own bedroom rather than your partner's.

"Her bedroom," he confidently answered.

I continued with the questioning. "And what time of day or evening would you say it was?"

"It's about midnight."

Point made? Jill couldn't believe what she had just heard. Jack, at least at this point, thought he had completely nailed the scene. Let's review Jack's scenario: he believed they had been dating for about two weeks and were in her bedroom at twelve o'clock midnight.

With Jack and Jill playing such different scenarios, how could their scene have ever worked? They had two different relationships, they had known each other different lengths of time, and they were in two different locations at two different times of the day. They just weren't doing the same scene. And it really doesn't matter what great actors they were; the scene was simply never going to work under these circumstances.

Since they were on such different wavelengths, I know you're wondering who was right. One of them must have had a better grasp of the scene than the other. You're probably thinking to yourself, "Why didn't the director get off his duff and give them some basic information?" The director—*moi*—didn't need to, because the very first sentence on the left-hand column of the page, where the directions are given (dialogue is on the right side of the split page in most commercial scripts), stated, "Two college friends who had met in high school a few years before, on a park bench in the middle of the afternoon."

I know you're thinking that what I've just described is some way-out, extreme example. *Wrong!* It's typical. This happens every day in auditions. Many scripts give some information, but what if, for example, there is no description of the characters? Then at least discuss the scene with your partner and come up with the particulars. Even if all of these questions are answered in the script, the two actors should still discuss it, because they probably still won't be on the same wavelength with regard to the interpretation of that information.

The Director's Role: Fixing the Scene

Even if you're both wrong, at least you'll be wrong together. A director can fix a scene that works, even if the interpretation is way off base. If an actor is consistently wrong, that's fine. That's easy to fix. The problem arises when an actor doesn't know anything about the characters and other particulars mentioned above, so each time he says a line it comes from different data. For instance, when he reads one line he might sound like the brother, in the next line he might sound like the boyfriend, in the next he might sound like the father, and so on. The reason each line comes out with a different interpretation is that the actor hasn't made firm decisions about the character and the situation. If he consistently sounds like the boyfriend even though he's not actually the boyfriend, a director can easily fix that.

Suppose you have a "ping" in your car that pings infrequently. There are no set intervals for the pinging—it just pings when it wants to. When you take your car to the mechanic, it's really hard for him to find what is making that ping, since it never pings when he's looking for it. But what if it pinged all the time? Then the mechanic would have no problem finding what was wrong since the problem was consistent. The same is true with a scene. Define the characters and the situation, and the scene will be consistent.

As another example, recently a man and woman came into an audition I was holding. The commercial was for a major television news network. The two were supposed to be news commentators. The commercial went as follows:

MAN: Hi. I'm Larry.

WOMAN: And I'm Susan.

BOTH: And we're here to tell you about XYZ News.

MAN: Susan, tell the great folks out there why our reporting is so phony.

WOMAN: Sure, Larry. It's because we're models and not real news people.

MAN: Yeah, Susie, we care more about how we look than how we report. Back to you, Susie.

WOMAN: And I'd like to add that our salaries reflect our good looks.

MAN: Say goodbye to the folks, Susie.

WOMAN: Goodbye, folks. (*privately to man*) That was real special.

MAN (*privately to woman*): Nice dress!

ANNOUNCER (VO): Unlike our competition, at XYZ we not only have real reporters, we report hard news.

When this particular man and woman read the script, something just wasn't clicking. There was something about the scene that wasn't right even though the actors themselves were extremely talented. I knew what the problem was. As I said earlier, when you have very good actors and an audition scene isn't working, often the problem can be traced back to the fact that they aren't doing the same scene.

So I started asking questions. The very first question told me what the problem was: "What is the relationship, or is there one, between the two people in this scene?"

The woman answered first. She said, "Well, it's obvious that they don't like each other. They are both trying to get more camera time during the entire scene. It's apparent that they are jealous of each other and probably fight on a daily basis about who is going to get the best stories. Just take a look at the last two lines. They are being so sarcastic to each other as they whisper those mean things. The part that makes the commercial funny is that the other television station, not XYZ, has nasty newscasters."

The man was stunned. The whole scene reminded me of the television program *Divorce Court*—you know, where the guy is always accused of being insincere, unsympathetic, uncaring, and a bad listener, and the woman is the type who watches *Oprah* and cries a lot.

He said, "Well, I completely disagree. Actually, they are crazy about each other. He is trying to pick her up, and she's going for it. It's obvious that they care for each other; just look at the last two lines. They whisper those sweet nothings to each other. It's funny because the newscasters here are obviously more serious about *each other* than they are about good reporting."

Huh? How can two people come up with such a different take on a script? How many times have you heard two people talk about the same situation and not agree on anything about the event? It's amazing to us directors why actors just don't take a few minutes to discuss a particular scene when given the opportunity.

So, let's review the basic particulars actors should always agree upon:

1. What is the relationship, or is there one, between the two people in this scene? Discuss the relationship in some detail. For instance, if they're married, do they have kids? Do they live in a house or in a cramped apartment?

2. How long have the characters been in this relationship? Discuss some particulars about the time frame. For example, if the situation is a dating one, does the relationship seem tired or fresh? Are the characters happy with the way the dating is going?

3. Where does the scene take place? Instead of just saying "A park," for example, discuss the surroundings. Are there any kids nearby, maybe on swings or other playground equipment? Is the weather hot or cold?

4. What time of day or evening is it? If it's in the morning, did you just get up? If it's in the afternoon, what did you do all morning? If it's in the evening, are you tired from a hard day's work?

These four basic questions about the type of relationship, how long it's existed, where the scene takes place, and what time of day or evening it is are pretty standard. However, your particular scene, which will have different partners and different situations, will obviously call for different follow-up questions to these basic four. But the point is clear: make sure you and your partner agree on the particulars of the scene.

What do you do if your partner is a "reader"? A reader is someone who reads a certain character with all the actors who are auditioning. Perhaps the reader already has the job and we're trying to see who plays best opposite her. Or perhaps the reader is a hired actor who is only there to read with actors auditioning for various roles. Sometimes we want each actor to have the same reader so as to give everyone the same set of circumstances under which to audition.

Even if you have a reader, you need to build a scenario in your own mind about the scene based on the four particulars stated above. When you arrive in the audition room, if you receive new information, fine. Then you can apply it. But at least have a game plan going into the audition. Otherwise, you're just reading lines.

You and your partner(s) are in this together. Help each other out. A candle loses nothing by lighting another candle.

Multi-Person Commercials

8

No snowflake in an avalanche ever feels responsible.

You have more obstacles when auditioning with a partner than you do when you're performing solo. Many times you have very little rehearsal time with your partner, and the unpredictable nature of the situation presents other problems, which I'll discuss now.

In the previous chapter I talked about how to reach the same basic understanding of the scene as your partner. In this chapter, we'll take that idea of being on the same wavelength a few steps further. Most of what we learn in real life is visual. What we see gives us more information than what we hear. For instance, if you're listening to news on the radio about a car wreck, you have some sympathy for the people who were in the car. However, if you *see* the injured people in the car on television on the evening news, you will probably have much more sympathy for their plight. This chapter will go into great detail about the ways actors relate to each other visually and physically.

Can an Acting Partner Ruin Your Performance?

Many acting teachers will tell you that you're auditioning for yourself, even if you have a partner. They tell their students that if they just worry about their own performance, they'll be fine—that the auditioners are judging you for you, not judging you with a partner. These instructors, whose ophthalmologists have obviously suggested marijuana for their glaucoma, believe your partner's performance isn't that important to you even if you're auditioning with a research cadaver. This notion is extremely ill conceived. I know it sounds "arty" to say that another person's performance can't affect yours, but the reality is, it isn't true.

What if your partner does for you what Goofy does for Disneyland? Can a partner actually bring your performance down? You bet! If you went to see a play with ten characters and nine of the actors were fabulous, but there was one who was horrific, whose photographic memory had no film in it—wouldn't that kind of ruin the entire play? If you put on a dinner party and nine couples are all conversing and having fun but one couple is yelling at each other, does that couple put a damper on the entire evening? So it's just a fact of life that when you have a partner, you have more things to contend with than when you're doing a commercial audition solo.

So what do you do if your partner is awful? One thing you should *never* do is put down another actor in an audition. You don't know who's dating whom, or who's friends with whom. In *How to Act and Eat at the Same Time: The Sequel,* I give a couple of examples where I have personally said something pretty negative about an actor, only to find out that the actor was related to the person sitting next to me. In fact, I have an entire chapter of the book devoted to this topic. I won't repeat the horror stories, but suffice it to say that when an actor puts down another actor, it will always come back to bite him in the end.

Here's what you *can* do: when the audition is over and you both start walking toward the door to exit, let the other actor go out the door first. When that actor is totally out of earshot, you can turn to the auditioners and ask, "May I read it with someone else?" Of course, ask in a very nice way. If the actor was that bad, we'll know why you're asking. If there are dozens of actors waiting in the lobby and we're an hour or so behind, use your judgment whether or not to ask.

Many times this is a judgment call that you won't get right. That's okay. You'll just have to wing this one, since there are no real guidelines. I can't give you the formula for success, but I can give you the formula for failure: try to please everybody.

Try to Find Out in Advance Who Your Partner Is

Usually, the casting director will tell you with whom you'll be auditioning before you enter the actual audition room. Sometimes each talent agency is given a block of time and the agents pair the partners together. Other times we have matched photos with actors that we think will look good together, based on the photos sent to us by agents. Another, though less common, way to do the pairing is for the casting director to just come out into the lobby and randomly start assigning actors to work together.

In any case, it's important that you try to find out who your partner is before you enter the audition room so that you can do the preparation work mentioned in the last chapter. One way to find out is to ask with whom you'll be reading when you arrive at the audition. Another way is to observe the sign-in sheet and use some common sense. If you're a male and the script calls for a male and female, look at the sign-in sheet to see which female has the same time slot as you. In other words, let's say your call-time is for 9:15 A.M., and you notice on the sign-in sheet that a female has the same time. Odds are you two might be reading together.

If all else fails and you can't find out who your partner is, or if everyone is going to read with the casting director or a reader who is already in the audition room, then just ask anyone who is available to read with you. Even if it's not the actual person with whom you'll be reading in the audition, at least you'll get to rehearse with someone reading the lines of the other character(s).

Study All Parts

Whenever you're preparing to go into an audition where you have a partner (or partners), it's extremely important that you at least look over the other part(s), assuming you're the same sex and about the same age as the other character(s). Frequently in a two-person scene, for instance, we'll ask the two actors to switch parts.

Sometimes we might ask one person to remain in the audition room to read a different part while dismissing the other partner. If you are dismissed in an audition while your partner remains, please don't necessarily take this negatively. Perhaps we're thinking at this point that we want to call you back, but we're not sure about your partner. Or perhaps you are so wrong for the part that we don't want to waste any more of your or our time. In other words, don't take this kind of dismissal to mean anything in particular.

The director might ask you to read another part for the sole reason of seeing how much range you do or don't have as an actor. I personally think this directorial technique has more validity when we're casting for a feature film or television show than for a commercial. For a commercial character you're most likely not going to have to have a wide range of emotions, since in most cases the characters in commercials won't need them. However, there are exceptions. Perhaps the director and client aren't exactly sure what they want in the character, so they want someone with a wide acting range. That way the director can try different approaches to the character on the day of the shoot.

Whatever the reason, if you're asked to read for another part, it's best to be prepared. So while you're rehearsing with your partner(s), you might suggest that you switch parts and give it a whirl, if the other part(s) seem fairly compatible with your physical type.

The Separation Problem

Almost all actors in auditions stand too far apart from each other. The camera actually separates people and objects on the screen. For instance, have you ever seen something on television or in a feature film and then actually seen it in person and wondered why it looked so much bigger on the screen?

A good example might be Elvis Presley's home or the White House. Yes, these two houses are big, but they look much bigger on the screen than they do in person. One thing I constantly hear from actors is that they worked with such-and-such a star and couldn't believe "how short and small he was in real life."

In auditions most actors stand at a normal distance away from each other. There is a comfort zone that people don't want to invade. But the problem in auditions is that if actors stand at a normal distance from each other, they will appear in playbacks as though they're on opposite sides of the room. So we end up with one actor on the far left of screen and the other actor on the far right. When viewing these auditions in playback, the director's eyes have to go from the far left to the far right of screen and then back to the far left and then back to the far right, and so on. The director's eyes are actually spending about 90 percent of their time on the wall behind the actors instead of on their faces.

However, if the actors stand shoulder to shoulder, they will close that gap. Yes, it feels kind of weird to the actors, as though they are all over each other. However, on camera it will look natural. Next time you're in a commercial acting class, watch actors who stand a foot or so apart and notice the actors who are standing shoulder to shoulder. The latter actually look more natural on camera, although the positioning feels unnatural to the actors. Make sure our eyes are watching you and your partner, not what's in between you.

Two-Person Slates

The general rule of thumb is that two actors should slate left to right, *as viewed on the screen.* This is the way we read, so it's a natural flow on camera. Notice that when you're watching a television show, commercial, or feature film, many things on the screen move left to right. Car chases, people running down a street, actors' entrances, and other such scenes often flow in this direction.

However, if we want something a little offbeat, the director might reverse the direction. Many times in sitcoms, for instance, people enter from the right to the left—again, as viewed from the screen POV (point of view). Think of some of your favorite television shows. It depends on the show, how offbeat it may be, and many other factors, but believe it or not, directors spend an enormous amount of time thinking about such things.

So directors are used to seeing actors slate from left to right from the screen POV. Keep in mind that the viewers see a mirror image of you. So although it will appear to the viewer that you are slating left to right, the actors should actually slate starting with the person on the right and then go on to the person on the left.

When you first enter the audition room, it is better if you can end up on the right side of the screen from the audience's POV. You're in a better position if your partner is to the right of you. According to my statistics, when dealing with a two-person commercial, the actor who was cast in my auditions was standing on the right side of the screen 69.7 percent of the time. Keep in mind that it is extremely rare to actually cast two people who read together in the same audition. Of course, this doesn't hold true in the final callback, since at that point we've already matched the people who could possibly be cast together in the actual commercial.

All studies have shown that in magazine ads, material on a right-hand page receives more attention than its counterpart on a left-hand page, all else being equal. In fact, many magazines charge more for an ad on a right-hand page than one on a left-hand page.

Since we read from left to right, our eyes are used to moving in that direction. As our eyes move from left to right, they will hesitate slightly on the right side before going back to the left, because going to the left feels like going backward. Because of this slight hesitation, the person on the right will usually get more attention.

Don't take this too seriously, though. You aren't going to cut your throat by being on the left side from the camera's POV. I'm just trying to give you every advantage possible when auditioning. Very few actors understand this concept, so you probably won't have to fight the other actor for that position. Try to walk in the door to the audition room first, if possible, so that you will be able to control who is on what side. Even if your partner enters the room first, you still have a fifty-fifty chance of ending up on the side you wish.

Slating Chemistry

When you slate with a partner, it is extremely important that we feel you two will work well together. The chances of your actually being cast with the person with whom you originally auditioned are extremely remote. However, it's important that you show us you work well together with other actors in general.

So when your partner slates his name, you should look at him and smile the entire time he is giving his slate. (Hopefully he'll return the favor.) So right from the get-go you're showing us that you have chemistry with other actors. Try this in your next on-camera acting class: have one actor slate to camera with the other actor also looking directly into the camera or looking at his script, then have the second actor look directly into the camera while the first actor does the same. Notice that the two don't seem to have any chemistry. They just don't seem like a good match.

Next take those same two actors and have one look directly into the camera for his slate, while the other actor looks and smiles at the first actor. Then, when the second actor slates directly to camera, have the first actor look at the second actor and smile. You'll be amazed at the different visual presentations here. Keep in mind that we start forming opinions about the actors long before they read the first line. When the actors look at each other during their slates, they start building a visual relationship immediately. The relationship begins even before any dialogue is heard.

Also, keep in mind that we will probably be fast-forwarding after your slate, so you want to make a favorable impression from the very beginning of the taping. I've seen so many auditions where both actors were turned directly to the camera and neither looked at the other. The client would then say to me, "These actors don't have any chemistry. Next!"

There is another reason you should look at your partner during his slate. As a director, I can tell you that eyes go to movement on the screen. If I want someone on the screen to stand out, I can add movement to that actor, and the audience's eyes will tend to follow the movement. So as you swing your head to your partner and then back to the camera, you are actually causing the attention to be drawn to you.

If the other actor slates first, wait a beat or two after he finishes before you slate. This is important when it comes to viewing play-backs. The reason is that after the person says his name, the director may want to check it off on his list of auditioning actors. Also, as mentioned earlier when discussing the single-person slate, there may be a quick discussion, just a few seconds long, about the first actor after he slates: "Wow, he has a real face for radio," "She's perfect,"

"I've seen prettier faces on a pirate flag," "She has lots of sites that call out for electrolysis," and so on. You don't want to be delivering your slate while they are discussing the first actor. Also, the camera must pan over to you, which takes a few seconds because the cameraperson will have to frame you up and readjust the focus. Often during playbacks we start to hear the second actor's slate during the swing of the camera, when the second actor isn't even on camera yet. But don't take this to an extreme. We shouldn't go from the age of consent to the age of collapse while you wait to slate. I'm talking about only a few seconds here.

Who Really Tells the Message in a Scene?

In television, feature films, and commercials, who really tells the message in the scene: the person speaking, the other person, or both, and why? Really think about this before responding, because the answer is one of the main bases on which directors edit scenes.

Some actors will say it's the person speaking. After all, they believe that the person delivering the dialogue is giving away all the important information; that's why the script is so important and why it's followed word for word whenever we shoot a commercial. Since most actors start out learning their craft on the stage, they believe the dialogue drives the scene. With regard to theater acting, those actors are correct. The audience is physically too far away to see an actor raise an eyebrow, for instance, or to even see many facial expressions. Therefore, theater audiences listen to dialogue very carefully to follow the story line.

Many actors will say it is both the person speaking and the other person, because one gives the message by delivering the dialogue and the other reacts to it. This isn't a bad answer. It takes two to tango, as we say. One actor takes from the other, and it is their give-and-take that presents the message to the audience.

However, the question was "Who really tells the message in a scene?" In other words, who gives the most information? In the screen world, the best answer would be, "The other person."

Let's suppose you're watching a broadcast of the Democratic or the Republican national convention. This guy is an incredible speaker, full of dynamite, and the audience loves every minute of his speech. But then the director cuts to someone in the audience who is nodding off. Then he cuts to someone flipping through the pages of a book, paying no attention to the speaker. Next, he cuts to someone yawning. Is the guy a good speaker now? No matter how great the speaker is, the reactions to that speech really tell the message: no one is taking him seriously, and he's so boring that sheep count him.

On the other hand, let's say this speaker is making no sense and could sue his brain for nonsupport. Maybe no one knows what his problem is, but the audience is sure it's hard to pronounce and untreatable. Perhaps he has set low personal standards for his speech and is consistently living up to them. But the director cuts to someone who is nodding his head up and down to signify that he agrees with the speaker. Then he cuts to someone who is clapping. The next cut is to someone who has a tear slowly falling down his face. Hey, this guy's great! It's true—the reactions tell us whether he is a good or bad speaker.

Suppose you're watching a comedian. This comedian tells a joke, and I, as the director, cut to a few audience members laughing. Then I cut to some guy looking at his girlfriend, laughing and nodding his head up and down. Next, I cut to a bunch of people clapping while smiling. I am reaffirming and validating the fact that the joke was funny.

Now, let's take that exact same joke. In fact, let's take that exact same footage. This time, though, after the comedian tells the joke, I cut to someone looking around the room and not paying attention. Then I cut to two people whispering to each other, oblivious of the comedian. Next, I cut to someone getting up and walking out of the room. Finally, I cut to someone who thinks this comedian will go far—and it's not a prediction, it's a request. Is the comedian funny now? Again, the reactions to the comedian tell us more about how funny he is than his monologue does.

Once I was on a 737 jet that blew an engine. It sounded like machine-gun fire, and the whole plane was trying to roll over—not a good sign. Think back to a time when you were on an airplane where you thought there was a problem and the incident was scarier than Mick Jagger. What was the first thing that you did? After praying, you probably started looking around the cabin to see what other people's reactions were. If they looked nervous, didn't that make you more nervous? On the other hand, I'll bet that if they acted as though nothing was wrong, you felt better.

So in the emergency with the 737 I looked at the flight attendant, who was holding a tray of food in her hands. This woman, who lacked any seat-side manner, didn't even take the time to set the tray down. She threw it on the floor and went charging down the aisle faster than the Road Runner. When she opened the door to the cockpit, the pilot said something to the effect of (I'm leaving out two words in each sentence) "Shut up. And sit down."

Ms. Warmth shut the door to the cockpit and sat down in that little jump seat that faced us. It took about twenty minutes for an emergency landing. Do you know what she did the entire time? She kept adjusting her seat belt. She didn't have the strongest grip on the situation. You might say her reality check bounced. Now, what do you think scared everyone on that airplane—the action, or the reaction to the action?

Theater actors realize that the audience tells them how good or bad their performance was. If the audience is moving around in their seats, coughing, talking, and so on, they know the show isn't going very well. Mind you, everyone in the cast could be giving the exact performance they have been giving every night of the show's run. But the audience's reaction changes every night, and that audience will "tell" those actors each night how well they are or aren't doing.

Stage actors see this phenomenon night after night during their performances. In fact, you've probably noticed that the comedy in which you performed was usually funnier on Friday nights than on weeknights and that it was the most humorous on Saturday nights. Which performances were the least funny? Matinees, of course. So the play seems to go over much better on weekends than during weekdays and to be more lackluster during matinees. It's the same play. But the audiences' reactions will tell you whether the play is any good or not during any particular performance.

Interestingly, theater audiences can, to some extent, shape your performance. Actors tend to put more of their souls into a play when the audience is appreciative. Actors sometimes fall into the trap of not caring as much about their performance when an audience seems uninterested. This is human nature. Rock bands, comedians, and street performers all seem to work just a little harder when the audience is on their side. However, as a professional actor, you should always give 100 percent no matter what the audience's reactions happen to be.

If you start watching television shows and feature films very closely, you'll notice that we cut to the person(s) reacting more than the person speaking. If you watch good situation comedies (which these days are much more situation than comedy), you'll notice that a particular line gets a laugh. But usually the reaction to that line will pick up the bigger laugh. The reaction to the line usually becomes more important than the line itself.

For instance, let's go way back in time. Remember the television show *The Honeymooners*? When Ralph was getting upset with Alice, even before he would say his famous line—"To the moon, Alice"—all he had to do was pull back his fist, and the audience would begin laughing. We all knew that that line was coming after he pulled his fist back. So it's not necessarily the line that got the laugh, but the visual reaction to the line that obtained the biggest reaction from the audience.

Another old favorite is the 1980s sitcom *All in the Family*. After Edith would say something intellectually challenged, Archie would slap his palm on his forehead, and then we'd hear Meathead flushing the toilet as Archie would roll his eyes. There would be an enormous amount of laughter coming from the audience. What got the biggest laugh—Edith's line, or the reaction to the line?

When Johnny Carson would tell a joke that didn't go over, he would turn his hands palms up, shrug his shoulders, and look at the band's drummer as he hit a rim shot. The audience would react with laughter and applause. Again, it was not so much the line that got the laugh, but the reaction to the line that received the audience's attention.

When David Letterman tells a joke that doesn't go over very well with his studio audience, he has visual reactions that save the joke. For instance, he might take his pencil, tap it on the desk, and then throw it behind him. The director will then put in a sound effect of glass breaking. The audience roars. Or he might tap the microphone a few times, implying that it must not be on. Sometimes he'll straighten his tie while making a funny face. Again, much laughter comes from the audience.

So in auditions we are watching the person reacting more than the person speaking. We can hear the person speaking so we're already getting his message, but by watching the person reacting we're *hearing* and *seeing* the message. As illustrated above, the visual becomes much more important than the auditory.

If you tell a woman, for instance, that her boyfriend wants to break up with her, the news itself is neither good nor bad. But her visual reaction to it will tell you how she feels about it. If she's wanted him to break up with her but didn't know how to tell him, her reaction might be one of relief. But what if she was very much in love with the guy and wanting to marry him when she heard the news? You might see horror and shock on her face. Her facial reactions are what really tell us whether the news is good or bad.

Visual cues are what we use in real life. Suppose I say to a woman, "No, honey, I didn't go out with Becky, she's just a friend," while nervously looking at the floor, scratching my forehead, and putting my hands in my pockets. Now, the dialogue says one thing, but the visual says another. In real life, which do you believe, the verbal or the visual? You got it—the visual. It's no different on the screen than in real life. They are both visual.

Notice that even during field interviews on television news programs the person reacting takes on importance. The director will cut a number of times to the person conducting the interview. In fact, often only one camera is utilized, and the director actually takes lots of extra time to obtain shots of the interviewer just reacting. Frequently this is done after the interview is over and the interviewee has left. The director feels—rightfully—that it's that important to have reactions to the statements being given by the interviewee.

When I'm shooting a television show or feature film, I will usually pick up some extra reaction shots for editing purposes. For instance, after I shoot the master shot, two-shots, over-the-shoulder shots, and so on (see chapter 13), I'll shoot the close-ups. Sometimes, after shooting a particular scene in close-ups, I might put the camera on an actor and ask for facial expressions showing such emotions as, for instance, happy, astonished, proud, angry, or confused.

I might also ask for visual expressions of such thoughts as "Oh, really?" "You don't say?" or "Oh, come on." The expressions I'll ask for are of course ones that would fit that particular scene. Then, in the editing room, I have a number of reactions I can cut to that the actor might not have given me when the scene was originally being shot. Wouldn't I already have those reactions if they were ones that would fit that particular scene? Maybe, maybe not. If there's any question about what works, I'll be covered by the extra shots.

Since many actors come from the stage, they downplay the importance of the visual. In fact, even most screen-acting instructors spend an abundance of time working on how to deliver dialogue. They teach their students all kinds of ways to mark up the script with symbols telling the actor how to say the lines. They spend many hours working on which words to punch. Many instructors spend an enormous amount of time working on tongue twisters to help actors speak clearly. This is all fine and dandy. However, very few classes spend any time on the importance of the visual reactions. And take it from a screen director—the reactions "tell" the scene.

However, this doesn't mean you should "make faces." Some actors tend to use expressions and reactions on their faces that are more exaggerated than they would actually have in real life, which makes them appear to be at that age where they're still making gifts out of Popsicle sticks. The rule of thumb is that you should basically do what you would do in real life. For commercials, *sometimes* we do want a *slightly* exaggerated performance, depending on the client, but, again, it has to be believable.

Reacting to Third Parties

You should react not only to the person speaking, but to the other actors involved in the scene as well. Scenes in auditions, and sometimes even in shoots, begin to look like a tennis match: all the actors usually look only at the person speaking. This makes things really difficult in the editing room. For instance, take the following dialogue:

SUSIE: Bob, how's life?

BOB: Not too good.

MARY: What do you mean?

BOB: Nancy is leaving me. She's in love with someone else.

Suppose, after Bob says, "She's in love with someone else," Mary looks over at Susie for her reaction. Perhaps they both already know that Susie is seeing someone else. In the editing room I would probably decide that it would be much more interesting to cut to Mary's and Susie's reactions to each other, rather than just the reaction of each to Bob.

Don't get caught in the trap of reacting only to the person speaking. Most actors do just that, and it very quickly becomes phony. In real life we always look around to see reactions not just from the person speaking, but from other people as well. Next time you're in a conversation with three or more people, observe how the parties all react off each other. Usually they'll react off the speaker as they also react to the other people listening to that speaker.

Building a Physical Relationship

Besides reacting visually to each other, actors in a commercial can demonstrate a relationship physically. For instance, if the relationship involves a mother and daughter, perhaps the mother could stroke the daughter's hair, rest a hand on her shoulder, reach for her hand, and so on. Some of these gestures won't be seen if the shot is very tight, but whether they are seen or not, they will help the actors relate to one another. If the relationship is between two lovers, for example, perhaps they could hug, kiss, or even do something as simple as glancing into each other's eyes. Two friends could nudge each other. The list of ideas goes on and on. The important thing is to not restrict the relationship to just dialogue. Physical relationships such as the ones described above can be extremely helpful in establishing a visual relationship.

However, it's very important that you inform your partner about certain physical reactions. For example, if you were going to kiss someone, it would behoove you to let your partner know and to find out in advance what that person thinks about it. Even if you were going to hug another actor, it would be best to discuss this with the other actor before you begin your commercial audition.

Give the Director an Editable Scene

Being able to act isn't good enough! Many actors can act. The question that floats around in many directors' heads as you're auditioning is, "Can I edit what these actors are doing?" It really doesn't matter how great a performance might be; if I can't edit it, then the scene is unusable. Yes, there's an editor on shows, but remember it's the director who sets up the shots that will most likely determine most of the editing. And many directors sit in the editing room making most of the editing decisions. A number of directors have "final cut," meaning that in the end the show will be cut the director's way.

A lot of actors don't understand anything about the editing process. They naively believe that technical problems such as editing aren't really their concern. These misguided souls, who could get lost riding an elevator, couldn't be further from the truth. Unfortunately, it goes back to their training. Few acting instructors understand the editing process, so the knowledge doesn't usually get passed down to actors during their on-camera training.

Let's suppose actor A says to actor B, "You know, you're really a jerk, and I can't stand to be around you." Then actor B says, "You know what? Of all the people I've ever met, you are the absolute worst excuse for a human being."

In the editing room the director will probably cut the scene this way: the shot will be on actor A as he says, "You know, you're really a . . . ," but before he says, ". . . jerk, and I can't stand to be around you," the screen will cut to actor B for his reaction. Then, the shot will remain on actor B as he says, "You know what? Of all the people I've ever met . . . ," but before he says, ". . . you are the absolute worst excuse for a human being," the screen will cut to actor A for his reactions.

This is basically how we directors cut scenes. It's pretty standard to initially cut to the actor who is speaking and then cut to the person reacting while the speaking actor continues. The routine is then reversed for the actor who wasn't speaking. So it's extremely important that you always be "in the scene" visually when shooting a commercial, or for that matter, when you're auditioning. This is one reason visual relationships are so important.

The problem is that most actors have their heads buried in their script the entire time their partner is speaking. They believe that the right time to glance at their script is while the other person is speaking, since they have this weird notion that we're not watching them at that point. It would be best, when speaking dialogue, to alternate between glancing at your script and glancing at the other person. It is perfectly okay to sometimes glance at your script while the other person is speaking. Just don't do it during every speech the other actor delivers. And there's nothing in the rule book that says you can't still be reacting while you're glancing at your script as the other person speaks. It's puzzling why actors' faces sometimes go completely blank when the other person is speaking and they're looking at their own script.

While you're glancing at your script as the other actor is talking, be sure your facial expressions aren't mimicking what you're actually reading to yourself! Believe it or not, this is very common. Since you're most likely reading different lines to yourself than the ones your partner is speaking, your reactions would be inappropriate.

Also, it's important as you are reading those lines to yourself that your lips not be moving. It looks bizarre and makes the scene become totally unbelievable. Do actors do all these things in real auditions in New York and Los Angeles? *Absolutely!* I wouldn't put this material in this book if I hadn't seen it over and over again in auditions in the major markets with well-known and well-trained actors.

Listening

When I was an actor, way back when I was so young that I wasn't yet concerned with what diseases my ancestors had, I was in New York performing in a play when one of the actors made an entrance and started to recite the lines from act 3. This would have been fine had the actor been sober and had the rest of the cast been in act 3. Unfortunately, he wasn't, and we weren't: the play had just begun, and we were in act 1. Since this actor had given the plot away before I could usher him offstage while ad-libbing, "Time for bed, Grandpa," we were in deep trouble. Not only had he had a little too much to drink, but he was so old that he was at the age where you realize your father was right—the world really is going to hell in a handbasket.

Now, the other three actors and I had two more hours to fill, and the audience already knew the outcome. I learned something very important that night: the art of listening onstage. As an actor I had always been told that you have to listen carefully to what the other actors are saying even if you know everyone's lines by heart; otherwise your reactions will be fake. That night I *really* had to listen and concentrate on everything the other three actors were saying so that I could ad-lib with them. Though I can't speak for the story line or dialogue, I can tell you that on that night we actors gave our most believable performances of the entire run of the show.

You and I know that in real life people play off each other. We react in accordance with how the other person speaks to us, as well as to the words he uses. In everyday life we listen to what the other person is saying, interpret what he has said, and quickly decide how we're going to visually react to it. We listen with our eyes as well as with our ears (i.e., we watch his face, body, hands, etc.).

The first step, then, in visually relating to your partner in any type of acting performance is *listening*. When you are relating to your partner, if actor A says a line to you, you'll react one way, whereas if actor B says that same exact line to you, you'll react another way—because actors A and B aren't delivering the line to you in the same manner. Again, you must play off each other. Otherwise, we have two actors simply reading lines to each other, giving their own separate performances; there's no real communication between them.

A good exercise is to pick up a script neither you nor your acting partner has seen before. Have your partner read one character's line or lines, then make up a line or lines to fit his line(s). Then have your partner read the next line(s) for his character in the script. Continue to make up lines that would fit your character in that scene. In other words, only your partner will read the lines from the script. You'll have to fill in the gaps. In this exercise, it's not important whether or not you fill in with sentences like the ones in the actual script. The essential thing here is that you learn how to listen carefully to your partner. You will really have to relate to him in order to make the scene work.

The Importance of Partner Chemistry

At the beginning of this chapter, I discussed the importance of slate chemistry. The slate gets us into a mindset about how much chemistry there is or isn't going to be between you and your partner. That chemistry needs to continue throughout the rest of the scene.

Basically, when it comes to casting, it's not a matter of how good you are individually. It's a matter of how good you are with another person. Let's take one of my favorite bands: the Beatles. They made hit after hit and are now considered to have been among the music world's greatest pioneers. Together they just couldn't be beat. Individually, though, they haven't done as well. They were much better together.

Think back to some of your favorite sitcoms. Where are most of those actors today? They were great as an ensemble, but individually they probably aren't as good. Think of all of the sitcom stars who have gone on to make movies that failed or who have starred in other television shows that left you wondering what happened to their talent. Nothing actually happened to their acting skills. It's just that they were good with their co-stars in the show you liked, but not necessarily with other people.

There are so many films that have failed despite having major stars who are terrific actors. It's not that those actors lack talent. It's just that the pairing didn't work. You might know this from dating or marriage. You're definitely better with one person than another.

As a director, I can tell you that this is one of the biggest challenges in casting. If I individually cast the best actor for each role, I would probably have a disaster on my hands. I have to cast the right person for each part, keeping the ensemble in mind. Being a good actor in and of itself isn't good enough. You have to be good with and off of the other actors. (I dealt with that in the last chapter, when I discussed how important it is that you and your partner make sure you're both doing the same scene.) It's extremely important that you have rapport with the actor with whom you're auditioning, which is why it's so important to have chemistry beginning with the slate.

Reading from Your Partner's Script

It is distracting when your head swings back and forth from your script to your partner and then back to your script. When two actors' heads are swinging, it doubles the problem. As you know, bobbing heads on camera distract from the performances of the actors. Yes, the constant movement of your head catches our attention, but a constantly bobbing head catches our attention for the wrong reason.

Here's a trick you might want to think about employing: try reading from your partner's script. It helps if your partner angles his script toward your face. You can pay him the same courtesy. You won't believe how much less head movement you'll use with this technique. The reason it works so well is that you'll have far less head movement from your partner's script to his face than from your script to your partner's face. If you're confused about why this is so, tape yourself and another actor while employing this technique and the reason will become very apparent.

Of course, it's best to work this out in advance with your partner. Done correctly, this technique can really improve both your performances. It also helps you relate to your partner more because you need to make only a small head movement to take your eyes from your partner's script to his face. When both actors do this, it's impressive on camera.

Pacing the Scene with Another Actor

One of the main problems with multi-person commercials is that the actors put one perfect beat in between every exchange of dialogue from one actor to the other. You couldn't do this in real life even if you tried. Try an experiment in one of your acting classes: ask two people to ad-lib dialogue back and forth and to put one perfect beat in between every exchange. Tell them that they can speak for as long or as short a time as they want, but that when one person is through with his dialogue, the other should wait one perfect beat and then deliver his line(s). I don't mean two or three beats; I mean one perfect beat.

You'll immediately find that in real life people sometimes wait three or four beats between exchanges of dialogue. Often they want to digest what the other person is saying, so they think for a few seconds before replying. Sometimes they have zero beats between exchanges of dialogue: they already know what they're going to say, so they just jump right in. And occasionally, yes, they have one perfect beat in between an exchange. But they *never* have one perfect beat in between *every* exchange of dialogue. Unless, of course, they're acting!

So make sure your dialogue is somewhat irregular, which will make it sound real; make sure you're talking like real people, not like actors who place one perfect beat in between every exchange of dialogue. Again, we get back to listening. Next time you're watching two or more people engaged in conversation, listen carefully to the pacing between the different exchanges. Why haven't you noticed this irregularity before? Because it's too natural; why *would* you notice? But if people in real life did put one perfect beat in between every single exchange of dialogue, you would notice, because it would sound so unnatural. Keep in mind that if it's not believable in real life, it most likely won't be believable on the screen.

The only time in an actual shoot that you can't overlap dialogue is in a close-up in which only one actor is seen (also known as an "isolation shot," because the actor is isolated—no one else is on camera at that point). In all other shots it is permissible, and often advisable, to overlap some of the dialogue.

The reason you shouldn't overlap dialogue in a close-up during an actual shoot is for editing purposes. For instance, let's say that in a particular scene we shoot all the shots leading up to the close-up, and you overlapped at *about* the same spot every time—no problem. However, in the editing room, when it comes to the isolation close-up, I'll have a real problem every time I want to cut to that close-up. It's possible that when I do make that cut we can hear your overlapped line twice, since it's impossible for the actor to overlap at the exact same spot every time. You'll be off one way or another by at least a beat or two. So why have actors overlap in a close-up when you won't even be seeing the other actor(s) on camera?

The director, if he knows what he is doing, will ask you to have "clean dialogue" in the close-up. When he gets into the editing room, he can cut from any shot containing the overlap to a close-up with no overlap. Then the director or editor can go back and manually overlap the dialogue (taking the track of the overlapped dialogue from another shot) and use it in the close-up. That way the overlap will occur exactly at the same spot.

So when the shot cuts, for instance, from the master shot (a wide shot containing all the action, explained in chapter 13) to the close-up, you won't hear the overlap twice and in two different places. Again, overlapping is only a problem in close-ups in an actual shoot. If it were a multi-camera shoot, then overlapping close-ups most likely wouldn't be a problem.

Don't worry about this in an audition. I only mention it for when you will be in an actual shoot. The audition should look as natural as possible. This doesn't mean that with all commercial scripts there will be natural places to use overlaps. You'll see more overlaps in television shows and feature films, where they are used constantly—far more often than in commercials.

However, you *might* find places to use overlaps in commercials. Let me repeat, because this is so important: *don't put one perfect beat in between every exchange of dialogue.* It's okay to have one perfect beat between some exchanges of dialogue, but when you have one perfect beat in between each and every exchange of dialogue, it will eventually sound phony.

Anticipating Your Partner

One thing that really shows an actor to be an amateur relates to anticipating your partner. When an actor doesn't say his line after one perfect beat but instead waits two or three beats, his partner will tend to look at him with an attitude of "It's your turn, igmo, speak." How does the actor know it's his partner's turn? In real life, we don't have "turns."

Be extremely careful that you don't fall into this trap. I've even seen this sort of thing in the editing room, where it's more annoying to a director than the kid on the elevator who pushes all the buttons. Yes, if you did this sort of thing in the actual shoot it would be my fault because I'm the director and am responsible for everything that happens on that set. But you could help us directors out! Again, the key here is to start watching people in everyday conversations. They don't nudge the person with whom they are speaking when it's the other person's "turn" to speak. They don't make funny faces, hinting to their partner that it's "his turn." So don't do it while performing a commercial.

It would behoove you to read some books on directing for the screen. The better informed you are about the director's problems, the more likely it is that you're going to be able to show him in your audition you're the right person for the job. In the next chapter we're going to continue discussing editing problems that we directors look out for while viewing your audition and evaluating your skills as an on-camera actor.

Openings and Closings

9

The scene most winning has its end close to the beginning.

It's extremely important that actors understand the editing process. It amazes me how many actors don't understand the basics when it comes to having their performance put on the screen. Many commercial acting classes teach the actor how to perform. Giving a good performance in a screen audition is important. But if we can't put that performance on the screen, it's useless.

Remember how your speech teacher in high school—the one who could've listed Karl Marx as a reference on job applications—drilled into your head that you need a beginning, a middle, and an end to your speeches? You've heard this more times than Liz Taylor has been married. The same applies here.

The Opening Shot

Let's start with the very beginning of the actual performance, which follows the slate. Most actors jump right into a scene and right out of it. Have you ever noticed that in real life people always visually react before they speak? They almost always have some kind of facial expression before they open their mouths. Watch two people in conversation and you'll see this routinely. However, when it comes to actors, you'll rarely see a visual opening.

We directors expect at least a five-second visual opening before an actor speaks the very first line. Five seconds is a longer time than you might think, so make sure it's really at least five seconds. This opening is our introduction to your performance. It makes your performance look more real and personal and adds a terrific visual human quality to your commercial right from the outset.

Another very important reason for the opening shot is for editing purposes. Do you know how fast a cut is in 35 mm film, which is the format used for most national commercials? Hint: with 35 mm film, each second of screen time contains twenty-four frames. So if we cut a frame, that cut would be $\frac{1}{24}$ of a second long.

Now, let's imagine that you have no opening shot. After the director yells "Action," you immediately begin dialogue. You have given me no room at the beginning of your performance. Imagine that I'm going to cut that commercial into a television program. So we're going to cut from the television show to you immediately speaking dialogue, $\frac{1}{24}$ of a second later!

This is known as a "jump cut." It doesn't make for a very smooth beginning, and it makes the cut very choppy. Advertising agency people would like for the public to get to know you visually very quickly in a commercial. When you just jump right into dialogue, it's as though you are in the viewing audience's faces, trying to sell them something.

Watch television shows and feature films very closely. You'll notice that every time we cut to a new scene, there is a visual opening—the actors aren't usually speaking right away. For example, let's suppose you're watching a film scene where an argument is taking place between a wife and a very aggressive husband—the type whose neck is as wide as his head and who is so bold as to remove mattress tags without fear of legal consequences.

At the beginning of the argument, you might see the husband throwing up his arms and getting ready to walk out the door as we cut to the woman shaking her head. A few moments later, we cut back to the husband turning around and staring at his wife for a few seconds. The next cut shows her staring back at him. Finally, we cut to him giving her a menacing look as he commences yelling. That is more dramatic and more interesting than just immediately cutting to the husband screaming. We have visually set the scene before the actors started speaking dialogue. So when the first line is delivered, it will be more believable than if we had just jumped right into dialogue with no visual opening.

Take this commercial opening line, which is being delivered to another actor: "Boy, there's a kid for you! And as special as kids are, they all love Wheat Brand Cereal." Almost every actor will start that dialogue immediately after the director calls "Action." Try this: after the director yells "Action," look camera left (to your right) as though you are watching some kid play on a playground, shake your head in amazement, and give a little chuckle (a human quality!). A moment later look at your acting partner and say the line, "Boy, there's a kid for you! And as special as kids are, they all love Wheat Brand Cereal."

This opening shot would take about five seconds to perform. Now you have given the director options. You have certainly made his job easier in the editing room, and you've shown him that you understand more about acting than just saying dialogue. Also, you've shown him a friendlier side of the character than have other actors who just immediately jumped right into the dialogue. Try the above opening line again, and this time take out the visual opening. If you watch the two back-to-back in playback, you'll be amazed how flat the take is that has no opening shot.

Take this opening line: "You know what? I have hemorrhoids and I'm embarrassed to talk about it." How about opening with this: look straight into the camera, shrug your shoulders, look to the right and left as if you're about to tell a secret, then look sincerely into the camera and say, "You know what? I have hemorrhoids and I'm embarrassed to talk about it." Now try it without the opening. Tape it both ways, and again, you'll be very surprised how much more real and human the one with the opening shot will appear. And, just as important, the director will realize that you understand how to make a scene work when it ends up in the editing room.

Let's say two actors are playing husband and wife. The actor portraying the husband looks right into camera and says, "My wife and I bank at First Fidelity because we believe in security." Before he says the opening line, perhaps he could hug his "wife," give her a kiss on the cheek, and take her hand as he turns to the camera to say his first line. Doesn't this visual opening say more about the relationship of the couple than any dialogue could ever hope to?

To take another example, let's suppose you have to play a pharmacist. The visual opening could consist of, for instance, your character looking over a clipboard filled with papers. A moment later, you could pull out a pen and write on the paper on the clipboard. Then you could look up from the clipboard and begin delivering dialogue. This gives the "pharmacist" credibility. It also helps the actor to feel more like a pharmacist, since he is performing an action that a pharmacist might actually perform. And, more important to me as a director, it gives me editing room.

Think of some visual opening shots that you can perform with the following opening lines:

- ◆ "Hey, Jim, I'm really thirsty."
- ◆ "Susie, this coffee is the best."
- ◆ "My wife and I want to go on a vacation."
- ◆ "My son and I always use Fisherman Lures when we head for the lake."

Also, if you jump right into dialogue, you will leave me with no timing options. For instance, perhaps when we shot the commercial it only came out to twenty-eight seconds and I need thirty. I could easily have picked up the two seconds at the beginning (or end) of your performance if you had given them to me.

The Closing Shot

Additionally, we need closing shots. With the exception of the slate, the ending of any scene usually becomes the most important part of the audition because, most likely, it will be the most memorable. If you watch a feature film that has a terrible ending, doesn't that ruin the entire film? It's such a letdown that whatever happened up to the closing gets lost with that bad ending.

Let's take the example of going on a blind date. Women: suppose this guy is the greatest. During the date he's kind, sweet, loving, considerate, spends a lot of money on you, wants to cuddle, stops and asks for directions, and listens to you (he doesn't exist), but at the end of the date the guy makes a physical move he shouldn't have made. Does that ruin the entire date? (We're supposing you didn't want him to make this move!) An otherwise terrific date could be ruined (or made even better) by what happens at the very end.

Women, let's suppose that, after making love with your spouse, he rolls over and immediately goes to sleep. Does that ruin everything that happened before the rollover? It really doesn't matter how great everything else was; if the ending was bad, the whole experience will be bad.

Suppose two actors are doing a dandruff commercial. The last line is delivered by the male actor, who says to the female actor, "So get in there and get beautiful with Balsam Balsam Shampoo. You'll be glad you did." Immediately after delivering that last line, most actors will look directly into the camera with an attitude of, "Hey, we're done."

However, what if after the line "You'll be glad you did," the male actor brushed the "dandruff" off the female actor's shoulder? What if he then shook his hand to get rid of the dandruff? Then the female actor shows embarrassment on her face. A moment later the male actor rubs his hands together to brush off the rest of the dandruff as he then looks at her with concern. The commercial now has a visual closing.

How long should the closing shot last? Five seconds, you say? You'll get the game-show buzzer if this is what you're thinking. A particular take is over when the director—or, in many auditions, the casting director—says "Cut."

In an audition, there's another reason actors should not cut the commercial themselves when they are through delivering dialogue. Sometimes the cameraperson will want to zoom in on each actor to remind the director and client what the actors look like in a close-up. Not only does the cameraperson have to readjust the framing, but he also has to refocus. Then he has to do the same for the other actor. This takes a little time. It would be better to continue the commercial visually than to just look into the camera with an "I'm done" attitude.

Some commercial acting instructors tell actors to look into the camera at the end of their performance so the auditioners can get a good last look at their faces. I can tell you this is a major mistake. If we haven't seen your face by the time you get to the end of your reading, you've probably lost us anyway.

Cutting Scenes Together

What if you have no opening shot and no closing shot? Now the director is in real trouble. "But, Tom," you say, "Maybe I won't have those shots in the audition because I don't know the script very well, but in the actual shoot I'll do all those things." If in the audition you don't give the director the shots he needs for editing, you won't have to worry about the shoot: odds are you won't make it to the shoot.

Let's suppose, for example, that you're a male and today we are shooting scene 3 of this particular commercial, television show, or feature film. Your last line to your female partner is, "You know, I love you, too." As soon as you mutter the last word, "too," you immediately look into the camera with an attitude of "I'm done, I've said all my lines, hand me my time card, I'm punching out." Or, instead of looking directly into the camera, you look over at the director with the same attitude. Now I have to make the cut on the very last word, because as soon as you stop playing the scene visually, the scene is over, whether I want it to be or not.

Now, let's suppose that the day before we shot scene 4. (We rarely shoot scenes in order, as explained in detail in chapter 13.) Your first line to your female partner is, "We should go to Jewelry Plus for the wedding ring." When I call "Action," you immediately start delivering your line. So where do I have to make the cut at the beginning of scene 4? I have to make that cut right on the first word, because you have given me no other option. You're making editing decisions for me.

In the editing room I now have to edit scene 3 and scene 4 back-to-back. This means that we're going to end dialogue in scene 3 and begin dialogue in scene 4, 1/24 of a second apart. You guessed it. We definitely have a "jump cut" here.

As a good example, think of a regular sheet of paper that measures 8½ by 11 inches. Perhaps I need to "edit" it down to a smaller size. But let's suppose you started typing words at the very top of the page and typed all the way down to the very bottom. I can't cut that sheet of paper without cutting into words on the sheet because you have given me no room to make that cut. Think of cutting the sheet of paper as editing.

"But, Tom, you're the director—it's up to you to make sure we give you what you need in the editing room." You know what? You're correct. However, this philosophy will get you cast about the time your descendants outnumber your friends. If you'll do your part, you'll make it easier for directors, who, in turn, will have more incentive to hire you. The fact is, not only will you make our job easier and your performance better with opening and closing shots, but you're also showing us how much you do or don't know about being an actor in the screen media.

Let's suppose, for example, that you asked me to drive you to the airport. I answered in the affirmative. You then said, "Here are the keys." What if I asked you, "What are keys?" You don't need to have any further conversation with me about my knowledge of driving. The keys are such an integral part of driving an automobile that if I don't know what keys are, you can be confident that I know absolutely nothing about driving a car.

Using human qualities, opening shots, and closing shots in your performance is such an integral part of screen acting that if you don't have those things, we think you know nothing about what an actor should know while on an actual shoot. It makes us wonder what else you don't know about acting and set procedures.

This concept of the opening and closing shot should also be applied to single-person commercials. You're probably wondering why I'm bringing this up now in the two-person section, rather than in the single-person-commercial section covered earlier. You have a point! The reason is that it is easier to understand the opening and closing shots with two-person commercials and then apply that knowledge to single-person commercials.

We need an opening and closing shot for single-person commercials for the same reasons we need them for two-person commercials: (1) making the scene more visual and (2) editing. The opening shot doesn't have to last at least five seconds, as it should with a two-person commercial, but it should last at least a few seconds.

Take the following single-person-commercial opening line, delivered directly to the camera: "Boy, did I make a mistake by not buying that new Supra automobile."

Perhaps before you say the line you could shake your head, kind of chuckle, roll your eyes, and then look directly into the camera to speak that first line of dialogue. You have now given the viewing audience time to get to know you a little before you just jumped right into dialogue. Also, you have given some visual human qualities even before you started any dialogue—and remember that a lack of human qualities is the number one complaint about your performance. Additionally, you have shown the director that you understand something about the editing process.

A closing shot is also needed for single-person commercials. Some commercial directors refer to this single-person-commercial closing as a "button." You'll hear that term used frequently in the industry. It's called a "button" because when you fasten the last button on a coat, for example, you are finished buttoning the coat. It's the last thing you do when putting on that coat.

Let's take the following closing line: "So, by not buying the Supra, I made the mistake of my life." After delivering the line you could gently throw your hands up, slowly shake your head back and forth, chuckle, and smile, looking right into the camera. Many actors think the commercial ends when the dialogue does. But you now know that it ends with the closing reaction shots, whether it's a multi-person or a single-person scene. Observe how people react when they are talking to you and have finished with their side of the conversation. You'll get great ideas for closing shots.

After finishing dialogue in a single-person commercial, many actors will look over at the person running the camera, roll their eyes because they weren't happy with their own performance, or even walk off-camera to leave. You can see how unprofessional this is and how little these actors understand about the editing process.

Playing the Visual Environment

10

The average woman needs more beauty than brains because the average man can see better than he can think.

Way back in history, before words were spoken, people communicated visually. And even now, we think visually. We think in pictures. Suppose you were to describe a car wreck you had witnessed. The first thing you would do would be to visualize in your mind what you just saw. You'd see it in your mind first. Most people will turn their head a little to the right and look just above the person to whom they are speaking when they're thinking about and/or describing something. This is because they are visually imagining what they're describing, actually seeing the object or person in their minds. Interestingly, if they are left-handed, they will usually look to the left.

So, since we think in pictures, it stands to reason that we should act in pictures as well. In other words, you must play the visual environment of the scene. You will play a scene differently depending on the physical surroundings.

Kids have a natural ability to do this. Ever notice how they can take any object and make believe it is something else? They can create an entire environment out of nothing. Well, most kids, that is. I remember once seeing one of my sons, who was almost four at the time, playing in a cardboard box. He was making all kinds of sounds while moving around in the box.

I asked him, "So, is this box an airplane?"

"No, daddo," he replied.

"Is it a car?"

"No, daddo," he again replied.

"Well, what's it supposed to be?"

"It's a box. Can't you see that it's just a box?"

The reason most actors play scenes auditorily and leave out the visual is that they are used to acting on the stage. After all, where do most actors get their training? You can't really practice your acting skills on network television or in a feature film. And since most actors who are working in Los Angeles, for example, come from smaller cities around the world, they don't have much access to working in the screen media.

Getting your training on the stage is not necessarily a bad idea. Actors can learn so many things about the profession by beginning onstage. For one thing, onstage they can hone their skills without ruining their careers. Few people, if any, will remember a play you performed in some small theater in Atchison, Kansas, for example.

However, do a bad performance in a feature film or on a network television show and we're talking about a whole new ball game. Because of reruns, that performance could haunt the actor for the rest of his life and thereafter. So I'm a big believer in beginning a career onstage, especially for actors who want to act in commercials, since both forms take a lot of energy.

Giving a Visual Performance

When you begin acting for the screen, not only should your facial expressions show you can play a scene visually, but your entire performance should go much further visually. For instance, let's say I'm shooting a scene with two people who are watching a football game. Suppose these two people only talk directly to each other and never watch the game, never look at the scoreboard, never watch a peanut vendor walk by. This is what the majority of actors will do in an audition.

At some point, the above scene would become totally unbelievable. In real life, these two people would visually react to what is going on around them. They might look toward where the game is being played, then observe the scoreboard, a vendor, other patrons, and so on. But not most actors! For some reason, actors just want to talk to each other, without regard to their surroundings.

Have you ever seen a feature film or television show where two people are in a car and the person driving is oversteering the entire time? You're thinking to yourself, "You Kato Kaelin freeloader, no one drives like that. Your car is all over the place." At some point, you no longer believe the scene. In fact, you're not even listening to what the actors are saying anymore. You are so distracted by the unbelievability of the visual that the scene itself becomes unbelievable. You just can't get past the fact that the scene is not working visually.

Maybe you've seen this same scene, but this time the Mr. Potato Head driver never looks at the road. Is it just me, or does this drive you nuts? God forbid that an actor would have to actually drive the car and act at the same time, so we might perhaps take the wheels off the car, put it on a flatbed truck, and tow it. This way the viewer will see the background moving by and believe that the actor is actually driving the car. Or we might hitch a tow bar to the car and have a camera truck tow it. The result is the same: the actors usually don't have to actually drive the car.

When a scene doesn't work visually, you no longer pay any attention to its meaning. You're probably thinking to yourself something along the lines of, "Please sir, you medical-research specimen, look at the road. I mean, my kids could be running across the street. *Please* look at the road." Again, you just can't get past the fact that the visual isn't working—the actors aren't playing the scene visually.

During my acting seminars, one of the scenes I give to the participants involves three people in a restaurant. They are discussing how
nervous they are because hit men are after them. It's very clear from
the dialogue that they are surrounded by hit men, with such dialogue
as "The hit men are only inches away from us" and "The hit men are
after us." It doesn't get much more obvious than that! No, it's not great
dialogue; the lines are from one of the most popular daytime serials,
one that has been playing on television since the days when people
thought Milton Berle in drag was hilarious.

I even explain to the participants in the seminar that the characters
are very paranoid and should keep looking out for the Mafia. One of
the lines in the scene is, "I have to keep looking around the room to
see how many faces the enemy has and getting so I can spot them."

Of course, what happens when they perform the scene? Ninety-
nine percent of the time, all three actors look *only at each other* the
entire time and never look around the restaurant. They're not playing
the scene visually. In real life they would subtly be looking around
the restaurant in a paranoid way.

Also, when most actors do this scene, they talk in a normal voice,
as three people would do in a restaurant. What they forget is their
environment. They are in a restaurant, surrounded by hit men; therefore, they should be whispering to each other. You must think about
what surrounds you when playing a scene, for reasons not only of
visual reactions, but also of volume. The physical surroundings will
change how you perform a scene. You would speak differently, in
terms of volume and other parameters, if you were performing a scene
on a school playground rather than during a church service.

Directors need actors to play scenes visually not only because
that's what people do in real life, but for editing purposes. I'm going
to need to cut to some of those Mafia people in the restaurant to
make the scene more exciting visually. As a director, can I cut from
three people talking to each other in a restaurant about Mafia people

to some close-ups of the Mafia guys, and then cut back to the three actors talking to each other, and so on? Yes, I can, but it's jarring. At some point it almost begins to look like our three actors and the Mafia guys are in two different locations. There is a disconnect because I haven't really tied them together in the same location in the most effective manner.

What I really need to do in the editing room is cut to one of our three actors looking out toward the Mafia men in the restaurant. Then I can cut directly from that actor's POV, seeing the Mafia people mingling in the restaurant. Next, I can cut back to that same actor as he turns back to talk to the other two actors. Utilizing this common technique, I have now connected our three actors with the Mafia guys, showing that they are in the same location.

Of course, I can only do this if the actors play the scene visually, by reacting to what is going on around them. Keep in mind that a screen director views an audition differently from the way an agent or a casting director views it. Agents and casting directors do not have to edit scenes. They generally view a scene in terms of how believable it is. So do directors, but the director has to view a scene not only from the standpoint of believability, but also from the perspective of the editing room.

So how does all this relate to you, the commercial actor? Whether you're acting in a feature film, a television show, or a commercial, there is always a location. Remember from our earlier discussion that there are four basic things actors should agree upon before performing a scene: (1) what the relationship is, if any, between the people, (2) how long they've been in that relationship, (3) where the scene takes place, and (4) what time of day or evening it is.

In a commercial audition you will rarely, if ever, be in any of the actual surroundings that you'll be in during the actual shoot. Normally you'll be performing in an office or, at best, a small studio. Let's suppose that you're auditioning for a commercial that will eventually be shot on a busy street corner. But the audition is being taped in, say, some casting director's office. You must visually create that street-corner scene for us. We have to "see" you in those surroundings in order to believe that you're in that scene. Perhaps you could appear to watch some cars drive by, visually follow a child riding a bicycle across the street, and/or see some pedestrians on the corner. No, we won't understand exactly what you're watching, but as long as *you* know what you're watching, the scene will be believable, because people do look around and watch what's going on around them when they're standing on a street corner. You're creating the visual environment and helping us to see you in that commercial.

What's even harder these days is that you might be acting in front of a blue or green screen. Many, many feature films, television shows, and commercials now use this process. We shoot you doing things in front of a blank screen and then fill in the backgrounds later via computer. You might be reacting off animated characters that aren't even present. You might be walking through a downtown scene, looking at buildings and other sights, even though there's actually nothing there. When using a blue or green screen, you really have to work at seeing an environment that is invisible to you.

In an actual shoot you might have to react not only to people or characters that aren't present, but even to entire events. For example, let's suppose you have to react to a train wreck. Do you think we're actually going to take you out into a field and catch your reactions as we wreck two trains? We might, in the editing room, for example, cut to your reaction to the two trains about to collide, then to some stock footage (footage already shot that can be purchased) of a train wreck that is supposedly from your POV, then back to your horrified reaction.

When I was an actor, way back before all the names in my black book had M.D. after them, I starred in a horror film being shot at Paramount Studios. In one scene I had to look into an empty swimming pool in which a dead body was supposed to be lying. The director had me look into a pool full of water with no body in it while he shot my horrified reaction. Then a few weeks later, he found a pool that had already been drained, stuck an actor covered in fake blood down in it, and shot it from my character's POV. In the editing room, he cut from my horrified look to the dead body seen from my POV and then back to my horrified look. When I became a director a few years later, I realized this is a very common way to shoot and edit scenes.

These are just a few examples of an actor having to create an environment. You can rest assured that if you spend any time acting in television, feature films, and/or commercials, you'll be reacting to things that aren't actually present during the shooting. This is one reason we really watch how you create the environment in an actual audition.

If the script has visual directions written into it, it is imperative that you read them. A majority of actors skip this important task, which is apparent to us because they don't follow the visual directions. Granted, in an audition you won't be able to do all the actions mentioned because you're not in that environment. However, with some imagination you can create that visual environment.

Season and Locale

It's important that actors realize what season it is supposed to be in the commercial for which they are auditioning. Many Christmas commercials, for example, are shot in the dead heat of summer. Your visual reactions are different when you're in hot temperatures rather than cold ones. And even knowing the season isn't good enough. You must know the locale. Winter in Minneapolis, for example, isn't the same as winter in Key West. Again, visually speaking, you react differently in these different seasons and locales.

In summary, please don't negate the importance of the visual environment. You should be working on creating the environment in every scene you perform. In time it will become very natural for you to always think of what is happening around you. I find this creativity completely lacking in most screen acting classes, and therefore in most actual auditions.

Basic Camera Staging

11

People may forget how fast you did the job,
but never how well you did it.

Before you audition for a commercial, as well as before you shoot one, you should understand certain staging directions and techniques. It's not that you're going to stage the scene yourself once you are cast. But you are more or less on your own in an audition, and it's just a good idea to understand the basics. Also, when you appear to have a grasp of basic staging techniques, you appear more professional. It makes the director think you have done this before.

First of all, let's review some commonly used stage directions, which also generally apply for camera work. The term *upstage* is used to describe the area away from the audience or camera. *Downstage* is used to designate the area toward the audience or camera. These terms come from European theater, where many of the stages are "raked"—they start low at the edge closest to the audience and then gradually rise in height as you walk *up* the stage to the edge furthest away from the audience.

Stage left is to the actor's left as he faces the audience or camera, not to the audience's or camera's left. *Stage right* is to the actor's right. *Center stage* refers to the center of the stage or the centerline of the camera frame. These terms are common to stage, television, commercials, and feature films.

Downstage right is the area nearer the audience or camera and to the actor's right. *Downstage left* is the area nearer the audience or camera and to the actor's left. *Upstage right* is the area away from the audience or camera and to the actor's right. *Upstage left* is the area away from the audience or camera and to the actor's left. Again, these terms are common to the various genres.

The director may say to you, for example, "Move downstage right." Or he may say, "Move upstage center." If he uses these stage terms, you'll know the areas to which he's referring because you're professional enough to know your business.

Some feature film and/or television directors will use the terms "camera left" and "camera right." This terminology may confuse the beginning screen actor because it refers to a position to the camera's left and right, respectively, not to the actor's left and right. This is, of course, opposite what a stage actor is used to hearing.

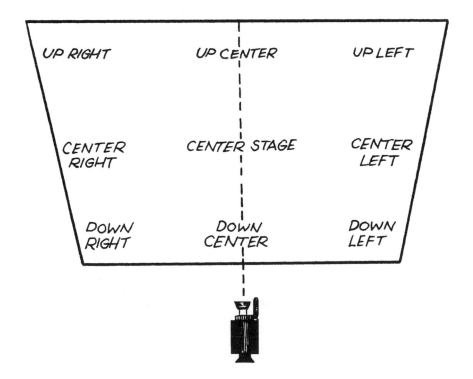

A screen director might also use the terms "move in" or "move out." "Move in" refers to the actor moving more into line with the centerline of the camera lens. "Move out" refers to the actor moving away from the centerline of the camera frame, putting him farther from the centerline of the lens, or even perhaps totally out of the frame.

The following suggestions are only that—suggestions. They are not rules that must be followed. When you're actually shooting a commercial, you should simply follow the instructions given by the director. Again, though, during auditions you'll be pretty much on your own. The director can get some idea of how much you've worked on camera just by your understanding of stage directions—your "screen presence." You've probably heard the term "stage presence." The same applies to the screen: if you have screen presence, you appear at ease and at home with the camera. Basically, you should keep yourself in front of the camera as much as possible and avoid turning your back to it unless directed to do so. If the director cannot see your facial expressions, he won't know how effective you'll be when dealing with the viewing audience. If you don't have good screen presence, you'll make the director's job much harder on a set.

Read the following ideas and suggestions and keep them in mind for auditions. If you know the rules of thumb, then you can break them whenever you find it necessary. But at least you'll be breaking them knowingly and not out of ignorance or naiveté.

Standing

For a majority of commercial auditions, or for that matter a majority of commercial shoots, you will perform standing up. This is because you generally create more energy on your feet than when you're sitting. You've probably seen the energy difference between a teacher who lectures standing up and one who sits in a chair; the latter loses fire. So if you're given a choice on an audition of whether to stand or sit, I recommend standing.

While standing—or in any position for that matter—watch your posture. Since the camera is focused in on the actor, any slouching will be greatly exaggerated. Keep in mind that the camera magnifies what it sees. Remember the discussion earlier about camera separation? If the camera sees good posture, it even looks better on camera. The opposite is also true. Bad posture on camera looks much worse than it does in real life. Also, bad posture doesn't put you in the best "spokesperson" position; you lose authority. You're giving the audience the impression that you're weak and insecure, as though you're the type that weeps openly during *It's a Wonderful Life*.

But, of course, there are those few exceptions when slumping might add to the character you're portraying in the commercial. If you were playing, for example, a character that had developed an unnatural fear of crossing guards, then the bad posture might be appropriate. Have bad posture only because it fits the character, not because you're too lazy to stand up straight.

It's usually best to stand with your weight evenly divided between both feet. The problem with standing with your weight on one foot and then shifting to the other foot is that when you shift, your face might go right off the screen. When you shift feet, your body does a slight dip, which could put you out of the frame lines. Also, the audience will see an up-and-down motion while you shift from one foot to the other.

Many actors don't realize how little space they have when working with the camera; a movement of just a tenth of an inch could put you on the edge of the frame or even take you completely out of it. During auditions the camera is usually focused very tightly on your face, so even if you lean on one foot and don't sway from side to side, you'll still look unbalanced. You don't project an image of confidence in this position. An even, balanced speaking stance is usually best. But, again, weigh the situation and then make your own decisions, depending on the character you wish to portray.

If you're auditioning with a partner, you want to avoid as much as possible standing with your profile to the camera. Profiles generally don't hold people's attention; the audience gets the feeling that you're hiding something, that you don't seem to be on the up-and-up. It's as if the viewers were listening to someone who is looking the other way. They just don't believe that person is being honest with them.

If you and your partner stand directly facing each other during the audition, the director will not see your faces and won't have any idea how well you react to another actor or to the message in the commercial. He will not learn much about your acting ability. What he will learn is that you haven't worked very much with the camera and that you don't really know the ins and outs of working with a partner.

If you're profiled, we won't be able to see around your face, unlike in theater, where some part of the face can usually be seen. Onscreen, if you are profiled we'll probably get a good shot of your ear. So it's important that you "cheat" to camera. Although your body should be facing the camera or maybe *slightly* turned toward your partner, you can turn your head to your partner to speak. But don't turn your entire body to your partner: if you do, you'll be in total profile.

As you can see from the illustration below, this stance will open up your body more toward the camera. You'll see a lot of this type of activity onstage and on television shows shot in front of live audiences. It's known as "cheating" your body toward the camera (or audience). Unlike what you might have done during college exams, "cheating" in our world is considered good acting technique. Even in actual commercial shoots, the director will often instruct you to "cheat."

BAD   GOOD

Upstaging

You and your partner should stay on the same geometric plane, neither of you getting closer to the camera than the other. In other words, you must be careful not to be upstaged. "Upstaging" means literally putting yourself upstage of the other person. Suppose your partner moves away from the camera (or audience), or upstage. You would have to turn your head away from the camera to look at him. Consequently, his face will be more toward the camera than yours. Remember, in an audition the camera is probably going to be placed directly in front of your face, so you'll be at a disadvantage if you turn away from it even slightly.

During auditions some actors will upstage other actors on purpose. I'm not saying this is a good technique, because if you get caught doing it you will look like an amateur and your partner will immediately become your enemy. That doesn't even take into account the ethics involved. However, some actors will tend to lean ever so slightly (though not enough to look off balance) on the upstage foot, putting them slightly upstage of their partner. If you try this, your partner will have to turn his head slightly toward you and you'll have the advantage. For one thing, the audience will see more of your face than his. For another, since his face is turned toward yours, the line of focus is toward you. I point this trick out so that you'll be sure not to let anyone pull it on you, not so that you can be discourteous to your fellow actor(s). If someone is a pro at it, he won't get caught. It will seem like a natural slight shift to the upstage foot, and he will not look off balance. But again, I believe there are ethics involved here.

As mentioned earlier, if you're auditioning with another actor, it's best to be on the right side of screen from the audience's POV. If you're auditioning with two other actors, it's best to be in the middle of the triangle rather than on either side, because the person at the apex of a triangle usually gets more attention. After all, the actors on the sides have to face in toward the actor in the middle when talking, and the lines of focus point to that middle person. And if the actor in the middle steps back just a little, he will cause the other two actors to turn even more sharply to look back at him. Again, I'm only pointing this out so that you'll be aware of it if someone does it to you. This is not to say, however, that you won't be seen if you're on either side of the triangle. You're going to have so much energy and do such a terrific job that you'll make yourself seen no matter where you are.

Am I saying that you should stay slightly behind the other two actors if you're in the middle of the apex? No, not necessarily. I personally think it's not very professional to upstage your fellow actors no matter how subtly you do it, but that's your judgment call. If someone does it to you, the remedy is to take a step back to counteract that actor's position.

Keep the scene "tight." Since the camera will automatically separate you, the shot will have to be pulled back so as to include both of you in it. The further the camera pulls back, the smaller your faces will become on the screen. Of course, while shooting the actual commercial on the set, the director will show you where to stand, but generally, as pointed out earlier, he won't give you much, if any, direction during the audition.

Sitting

Just as with standing, while sitting you also have to be careful that we see you and your facial expressions. If the commercial script requires that you sit at a table, for instance, remember that being behind (i.e., upstage of) it, rather than sitting on one side, will keep your face more in front of the camera.

If you're working with another actor, remember that profiles are to be avoided as much as possible. It's best for the two of you to sit at the back of the table together, which will open you both up to the camera. Sitting at the sides makes it harder to avoid profiles. Next

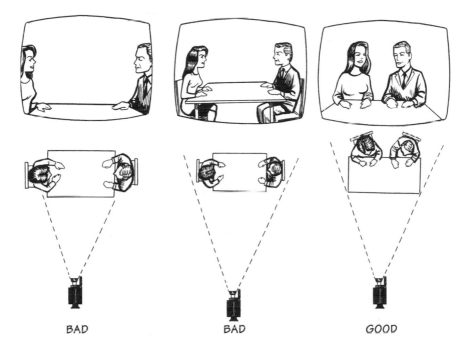

BAD   BAD   GOOD

time you're watching a sitcom or daytime serial, notice how the actors are positioned while they're sitting at a table. Sitting at the sides of the table would really put a lot of distance between the two actors, forcing the camera to pull farther back.

You'll also notice this type of positioning onscreen when a family, for instance, is conversing in the living room. Some actors might be sitting on the couch, with others behind or to the side of it. You won't find this technique used as much in other forms of filmed television shows or in feature films, because unlike sitcoms and daytime serials, they aren't shot all from the front, like a stage performance. However, keep in mind that in an audition the camera is almost always directly in front of you, no matter what the medium.

Be careful how you sit during the taping. Don't let your head pitch downward. While you are in transition between standing and sitting, don't let the camera see the top of your head. Keep your head and shoulders upright. However, don't take this too far. You should still appear natural and not stagy as you sit down.

While sitting, with or without a table, it's generally better to cross the upstage leg over the downstage one, rather than the other way around. This opens your body up to the camera. If you're sitting while talking directly to the camera, it really doesn't matter how you cross your legs. This is not to say, however, that you should cross them at all. You'll have to use your own judgment about what position best fits the character for which you're auditioning. Whatever you do with your legs, remember to be careful about your posture.

As with standing, when working with another actor remember to "cheat" toward the camera even though you're talking to your partner. The same techniques apply when talking to another actor while sitting as well as standing. If you are both sitting in chairs, don't angle the chairs to face each other. This puts you and your partner in complete profiles. For an audition, it is best to put the chairs right next to each other, both facing the camera, with no room in between. Then, when you sit, you can turn your heads to talk to each other, but we'll still see part of your faces. This may seem a little awkward the first few times you try it, but with practice it will become habit. Experienced actors do this automatically in auditions.

Some actors angle their chairs toward each other at a 45-degree angle. This is usually not the best way to do an audition: not only are you in a somewhat profiled position, but you're also putting a lot of distance between you and the other actor. To repeat, it's best to have the chairs facing forward and touching each other.

Kneeling

Rarely will you be kneeling in a commercial, but it does happen on occasion. If you're working with a child, for instance, who is much shorter than you and the situation seems appropriate, it might be a good idea to kneel next to him. If a child and an adult appear together in a commercial, the audience's attention is more or less automatically drawn to the face of the child rather than to that of the adult. For one thing, the child is looking up and the adult is looking down, so you can see the obvious advantage here for the child. Additionally, children just tend to get more attention on the screen (as well as in real life). Kneeling down to the child will help get you equal billing.

Since you want the audience to see as much of you as possible, it's better to kneel on the downstage leg, with the upstage leg bent upward. This position opens your entire body to the camera.

Some adult actors will cheat the child. When they kneel next to him, they will put their arm around him and nudge him forward slightly. This way, the child is being upstaged because he has to slightly look back toward the adult. I only mention this because I think it's incredibly unfair, uncouth, selfish, and just plain downright unethical to upstage a child in this manner. But, then again, there are some unfair, uncouth, selfish, and just plain downright unethical people in this business. Watch out for them. Unlike Noah, people who would do this have missed the boat. I bet in grade school even their imaginary friend left them for someone else. As punishment, perhaps they should be forced to watch one of those Jessica Simpson Christmas specials.

Walking

Remember that the camera will exaggerate your moves, so when walking try to keep your steps small. It's usually a good idea, in order to keep your body open to the camera, to start walking with the upstage leg rather than the downstage one. In other words, if you start walking from the left to the right as viewed from the audience's POV, it's better to start on the left foot, and vice versa. Eventually, you won't even think about this, just as you really don't think about shifting gears in your car. It will become automatic (pardon the pun).

However, please don't get too bogged down in this technique and think that you always have to walk this way. The point is, keep in mind ways to "cheat" your body toward the camera. This type of cheating is expected and very professional. It's just one more way an actor can show he has camera presence.

Be careful that you don't walk with your body pitched too far forward or backward. When your body is out of line (as with any posture problem), it will be exaggerated on camera. Unless the part calls for it, you don't want to look old enough to be debating the relative merits of Palm Beach versus Miami.

Crossing in Front of Another Actor

You must be careful not to turn in circles when you're crossing in front of another actor. If, for example, you were on another actor's right from the audience's POV and you crossed to his left from the audience's POV in the normal fashion, when you got to his other side, you'd have to turn 180 degrees in order to face that actor again and would then end up downstage of him.

To avoid this, it's best to first cross in front of him, stepping very slightly upstage just after you pass, and then turn around to him, resuming the normal posture for talking to another actor (facing the camera, as described earlier). Since you went slightly upstage of him, after you turn you'll be on the same plane. This may seem a little awkward at first, but like all other odd on-camera moves, this one will become natural with practice.

Whenever someone is crossing in front of you, you should make a "counter" move. This is a very small one-step move that you make in the opposite direction as the other actor passes in front of you. It's used to counter your partner's move, balancing out the screen. Many times a director will instruct you to use a "counter" when someone is crossing in front of you.

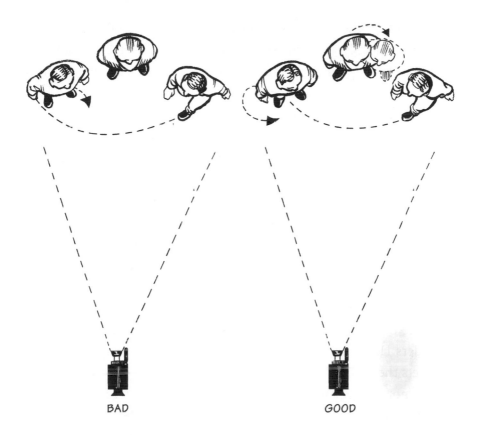

BAD   GOOD

For some reason it looks odd when one actor crosses in front of another and the actor who didn't do the crossing remains completely stationary. Let me point out that you'll make few such moves in commercial auditions because of the tight space, but it's a good idea to know how to handle a cross should you need to use one.

Head Movement

Having proper head movement is one of the reasons it's important for you to read the camera directions in the script, if they are available, before you start your audition. Often the script will inform you how close the camera will be on certain shots. However, while auditioning, don't take the instructions regarding what types of shots will be used too seriously. Keep in mind that most commercial auditions are shot in a close-up during a single-person commercial, while a slightly wider shot is normally utilized for a two-person commercial.

As mentioned in the discussion on cue cards, many actors tend to move their heads too much. This is a particular problem when you're speaking in an extreme close-up. If you're working with a partner, then the shot will most likely be wider so as to include both of you on camera, allowing greater freedom of movement; but you still must be careful to stay in the frame.

Another common problem is that of actors tilting their heads to the right or the left too much. I touched on this earlier when dealing with cue cards. If your head is tilted too much (and even a little bit can be too much), it will angle from the bottom corner of the screen to the opposite top corner. Aside from making you look like the type that considers Home Depot a place of worship, a tilted or bobbing head distracts the audience from your mission: to sell the product.

I'm not suggesting that you must always keep your head at a 90-degree angle to your shoulders. Certainly your head shouldn't be unnaturally stiff. The best thing to do is to practice with a camera and watch the playback on the monitor to determine exactly how much movement you can have with long shots, medium shots, close-ups, and extreme close-ups, which will be discussed in chapter 13.

Earlier I talked about using slight head movements while reading cue cards to make it appear you're doing less reading off the card than you actually are. Again, we're talking about *slight* head movements. Also, be sure to keep your head up and not tilted downward toward the camera. You'll need to be especially conscious of this on auditions, where the lighting will usually be very poor compared with the lighting used for the actual shoot. If you lower your head too much, you will get shadows under your eyes, and it will appear as though you are either tired or a suspected terrorist, or are the type that puts Jack Daniels on his most-admired list. On the other hand, don't angle your head up so far that the viewer will be able to see up your nostrils.

Another problem with leaning forward and/or backward is that it can cause you to go in and out of focus, which is very distracting. Many cameras used in auditions are put on auto focus, and just a slight forward or backward lean can create a focus problem. This is why we put marks on the floor for actors to stand on.

Also, leaning forward will make your head look out of proportion with the rest of your body, because your head will be closer to the camera. On camera, depth is somewhat lost. Therefore, it won't be that obvious that your head is closer to the camera than the rest of you, and you'll look distorted.

An exception to this forward leaning might be if you were going to place your hand vertically and perpendicular to your cheek as though you are going to tell a secret. Many actors lower their voices and lean into the camera slightly with this hand position. It's probably better to use this technique with no leaning, or very little, but there are, of course, exceptions.

Eyes

The eyes are extremely important in commercial advertising. You've probably heard the old saying that "the eyes are the mirror of the soul." In my opinion they are also the mirror of the commercial. Eyes are where truths and lies are revealed: "you can't hide your lyin' eyes."

There must be a lot of energy in the actor's eyes. They must be open and alive. A lot of amateur actors tend to squint when the bright lights hit them. Squinty eyes almost make it appear as though the actor has something to hide—definitely a killer in commercial advertising. The eyes should have a gleam in them. Many beginning commercial actors let their eyelids droop. Put some tension in your eye muscles and make those eyes "jump out" to the audience. Warm, bright eyes to a commercial director are like land to a drowning man.

When performing a single-person commercial, you'll probably be looking right into the camera, unless otherwise directed. Be careful that you don't have what I call "dangling eyes"—eyes that roam around aimlessly, not looking into the camera. Eyes should have concentrated focus. This makes the actor's words more believable and sincere. You must keep in mind that the camera is the audience's eyes.

How many times have you been talking to someone who was looking around the room for other people? Do you really get the feeling that that person sincerely cares about talking with you? If you're looking from side to side and up and down while talking to the camera, in effect you're talking to someone without looking at him.

When actors forget lines, they tend to roll their eyes to the top of their heads and look up to the heavens for help. God probably isn't going to bring the words down to you, and they aren't written on the ceiling. So if you forget your lines in a commercial audition, just keep looking forward, regain your composure, and go on. Looking up into the air just tells the people for whom you're auditioning that you're screwing up. If you just pause, keep your focus on the camera lens, and continue, they will at worst think you paused a little too long.

This isn't to say that if you use "thinking process" as a human quality somewhere in the commercial, as you should, you can't look off camera for a moment. In fact, perhaps it would look strange to not do so. However, there is a distinct difference between your eyes looking off to the side while you're thinking (as the character, not the actor) and having roaming eyes that lack any central focus.

Many actors, especially those just starting out, have the feeling that during the taping part of the audition they should be speaking to the people on the other side of the camera. This is a big mistake. As mentioned, on your initial audition, rarely will the people who are ultimately going to cast the commercial actually be in the audition

room while actors are present. Most likely, the people who will ultimately cast the commercial will see you on a callback and/or watch
the playbacks at a later time. If you're looking off to one side of the
camera, the people who watch the tapes later won't have the feeling
that you are communicating with them (and thus with the television
audience), and you won't come off as sincere.

There are some exceptions to this rule. Sometimes during the
taping part of the audition someone will ask you questions; if that
is the case, it's generally okay for you to look at that person as you
answer. On occasion the entire taping part of the audition might
consist not only of your performing a commercial, but also of your
answering some questions about yourself while the camera is rolling.
When that happens, look at the person who is asking you the questions, unless otherwise instructed.

Again, it's okay to stare off camera slightly as you "think" or react
to something that is off camera, whether it be another person or an
event of some type. You do this in real life as you talk to people. The
focus of your attention may be on the people with whom you are
speaking (i.e., the camera lens in a single-person commercial), but
you should occasionally look at something or someone other than the
auditor of your dialogue, as discussed in chapter 10.

Smiling

You'll probably have little chance of getting into commercials if
it appears as though you took smiling lessons from Dan Rather.
I touched on this subject earlier when dealing with the slate. In almost
all commercial acting, you can't overdo smiles. Keep in mind that I
said "almost." There are exceptions to every rule. Of course, you have
to read over the script and decide whether your character would be
smiling. But many, many times commercial characters are all smiles.

Smiles sell—big. And on a personal note: start smiling when you're young, because as you get older you'll want the crow's feet to go up!

Gesturing

Actors' gestures can be compared to people spending their first day at a nudist camp—what do they do with their hands? I'm not sure why it is that many actors say, "But what do I do with my hands?" I tell them, "Don't do anything." In everyday life, when you're yelling at someone, do you think to yourself, "Now what gestures can I use to show my anger?" You just use whatever gestures come naturally. You're concentrating so hard on what you're trying to communicate that gestures become second nature.

Some actors even mistakenly think it's a good idea to practice the gestures they're going to use while performing their commercial. You've probably seen speakers give a speech where their hands just didn't seem to match what they were saying. Many times a speaker's gestures are even a few beats late because he was concentrating on his hands and had to think about the gestures first.

You shouldn't think about what to do with your hands, nor should you practice what to do with them. Do you do this in real life? To repeat: in real life you just concentrate on what you're saying and what point you're trying to get across. Your hands will just do what they're supposed to do.

It's generally better to gesture with the upstage hand (the hand farther from the camera) rather than the downstage one if you're not standing directly facing the camera. Obviously, if you're working by yourself facing the camera, it really doesn't matter which hand you use. But when you're facing another actor, consider gesturing with the hand that will not cover you.

This isn't to say that you can't ever use the downstage hand, just that you should keep in mind the possible effect of upstaging yourself. Again, don't take this too seriously; it isn't something you should concentrate on. But with practice, in time it will become second nature.

Also, many actors think they always have to be gesturing with their hands. Nonsense! Again, we get back to observation. Notice that people aren't always gesturing during conversation. Use gestures as you normally would in real life if you were in that particular situation saying those particular words. I know you might be thinking that you aren't in that situation. True, but your character in the commercial is. And remember, you get your interpretation of that character from your own real-life experiences and from your observations of others.

Be careful about sticking your hand straight out in front of you and pointing at the camera. Because there's little depth of field on camera, this gesture will make it appear as though you have a short, stubby hand. Again, the camera "reads" very little distance between the finger and the rest of your body; it all appears two-dimensional. There are times, however, when it's appropriate for you to point.

As time passes and you become more experienced in working with the camera, many of these principles will become second nature. Just remember: though the commercial should contain a lot of energy, make that energy appear more in your face and eyes, rather than in big physical movements. You don't have to jump up and down and wave your arms. Energy doesn't necessarily mean external exuberance; it can also mean the internal excitement shown in your attitude.

Working with the Set

Learn subtle ways to "cheat" your body toward the camera by watching the way actors in commercials work with the sets. Sometimes you'll have to work on camera in ways that seem quite unnatural in real life but in a commercial appear normal. This section highlights a couple of the most common situations that you'll likely encounter during commercial auditions.

For example, when washing walls, windows, counters, and the like, it's best to turn your body toward the camera or about halfway from the wall to the camera. If you wipe the surface in the manner in which you normally would, your back would face the camera. Though that position may feel the most "natural," believe me when I tell you the audience won't think so!

When using a telephone, it's generally better to use the upstage side of your face instead of the downstage side. When you put the phone up against the downstage side of your face, you tend to cover your face. Also, it's important to keep the phone an inch or so below your mouth. This will open your mouth up to the audience and keep the conversation from becoming garbled into the phone. As usual, there are exceptions. For example, it might be that you are portraying a character who is placing a secretive telephone call. Then you would have reason to cover your mouth with the phone using the downstage side of your face. But then you must be extremely careful not to mumble the dialogue into the phone.

I would like to add a side note that really doesn't fit into the category of physical staging, but since we're talking about using a phone, it deserves mention. In a scene where you're talking on the phone, give the imagined person on the other end of the line adequate time to reply. Many actors rush through dialogue on the phone and fail to react to what is being said on the other end of the line. This is a true sign of an amateur actor who can't concentrate on the situation. Keep in mind from an earlier chapter that your reaction to dialogue is usually more important than the dialogue itself.

On the other hand, you shouldn't pause so long that the listener ages. But do at least allow enough time to make the conversation believable. It's quite rare that you'll actually hear someone on the other end of the line (either offstage or off camera); generally none of the phones on sets or stages actually work. It's up to you to make it look as though they do.

At the outset, the guidelines (they are not rules) in this chapter might seem almost as unnatural as the preparations for a colonoscopy. You will have to practice them many times before they become part of your repertoire. But in time, they will become more natural to you. You will have acquired what is very important to every actor in the screen media—good camera presence.

Script
Terminology

12

Most entanglements are caused by vocal cords.

*T*here are basically three types of commercials: spokesperson, slice-of-life, and voice-over narrative.

The *spokesperson commercial* consists of someone talking directly to the camera, pitching a certain product. This person represents the sponsor. Watch a few hours of television and you'll see examples of famous actors in spokesperson commercials. But this doesn't leave the beginning actor out, not by any stretch of the imagination. Stars actually compose only a very small percentage of the spokespeople used in the commercial industry.

The *slice-of-life commercial* consists of a short story that usually contains a beginning, a middle, and an end. In other words, the commercial is just a snapshot in time. These commercials are the ones you see where everything is resolved at the end because the people used a particular product. For example, the story might consist of a husband and wife who are having problems in their marriage because the husband doesn't like his wife's coffee. But someone comes to the rescue of their marriage with Folger's. All's well that ends well.

The *voice-over narrative commercial* consists of an actor who is on camera while the audience and/or that actor hear a voice that is off camera. An example would be an old man wearing plaid pants and a green jacket, the type who's still wishing John Wayne would come back, looking into the mirror thinking how bald he is becoming. Out of nowhere a voice tells him about a product that will spray-paint hair right onto his head.

All of these commercials basically fall into one of two categories: the hard sell and the soft sell.

The Hard Sell and the Soft Sell

The *hard-sell* commercial aggressively urges the viewer to purchase the product or service immediately—or else! An example might be the local used-car or carpet salesperson. They typically yell into the camera to try to get you to buy their product.

The *soft-sell* commercial demonstrates the advantage of the product or service without specifically demanding that you buy it, and generally does so in a friendlier, more relaxed demeanor. The message of trying to get someone to buy a product is subtler. Sometimes it's too subtle: have you ever watched a particular commercial and then wondered what product was being advertised?

With the possible exception of local markets, the soft sell is more common these days. Hard-sell commercials were used much more in the 1980s and early 1990s than they are now. Again, though, they are used frequently in smaller markets, so it would behoove you to learn this technique, even if you're working in a large market. Keep in mind that many regional and some local commercials are cast in the major markets.

Terms Every Screen Actor Must Know

The following list of the most common terms should provide you with a basic understanding of the vocabulary used in the average commercial script and audition and while on the set.

BG   Background; the area of the shot that is behind the main action. For example, in a script you might see, "In the BG there is a crowd of college students."

CGI   Computer-generated imagery; a term used for any effect that is composed in a computer.

CU   Close-up; a shot that is farther away from the subject than the extreme close-up, but closer than the medium shot. An example would be a close shot of an actor's face.

cut   (1) The joining of two separate shots so that the first shot is almost instantaneously (in $\frac{1}{24}$ of a second, in the case of 35 mm film) replaced by the second; (2) stop the action.

dissolve   A scene transition whereby one shot gradually replaces another. Often dissolves are used to show the passage of time.

ECU   Extreme close-up; a shot in which the camera is focused very close to its subject. This type of shot could be of a person's nose, mouth, hand, or foot, for example. It could also be of the product or product name. If the ECU is on any part of the actor, he must remain very still to stay in the frame.

EXT.   Exterior; a shot taken outdoors. An example in a script would be: "EXT. LEAR'S HOUSE."

fade   The process whereby the image onscreen gradually goes from light to dark, or vice versa. This type of transition, which usually takes place at the beginning and/or end of a commercial, is described as "FADE IN" if going from dark to light, or "FADE OUT" if going from light to dark.

focus-pull   Pulling the focus from one subject to another; taking something that is initially out of focus and bringing it into focus.

group shot   A shot containing three or more people or products.

hero   The actual product (hamburger, soft drink can, automobile, etc.) used in each take. For example, if McDonalds is shooting a Big Mac commercial, the actual hamburger used in each take is chosen from many "auditioning" hamburgers. The one chosen is referred to as the "hero."

high-angle shot   A shot taken from above normal eye level, down toward the actor or product.

INT.   Interior; a shot taken indoors. An example in a script would be: "INT. BARON'S BEDROOM."

loose shot   A shot that isn't very close to its subject(s). This sometimes refers to a medium shot (MS) but is more often used for a long shot (LS). You might hear the director say to the cameraperson something like, "Let's loosen the frame." This is an instruction to the cameraperson to widen the frame, which means he will "pull back" the lens.

low-angle shot   A shot taken from below normal eye level, up toward the actor or product.

LS   Long shot; a shot taken at a considerable distance from the subject. It could show a whole room or an actor's entire body.

master shot   A shot that usually shows all the principal actors in a scene. It is also known as the "establishing shot," since it establishes who and what are in a particular scene. Usually, it's the widest shot in any scene.

MCU   Medium close-up; a shot that is farther from the subject than a close-up, but closer than a medium shot. An example would be a shot of a person's head and shoulders or a shot from the mid-chest up.

MOS   Minus optical stripe, minus optical strip, or "mitout sound"; the recording of a scene visually without a sound track. An example in a script would be, "Woman washing kitchen counter (MOS)."

move in   Instruction for the subject to move in toward the centerline of the lens.

move out   Instruction for the subject to move away from the centerline of the lens.

MS   Medium shot; a shot taken at a greater distance from the subject than an MCU, but at less distance from the subject than a long shot. A medium shot of a person would generally cover the area from the waist up.

OC   On camera; anything that is recorded and seen on camera during a shot. An example in a script would be: "LS of Bob as Jim slams the door in the BG (OC)."

opening   The first shot of the commercial. For example, you might hear the director say, "The opening shot consists of you coming through the door, slamming it, and delivering your first line."

O.S.   Offscreen; actions or sounds related to the scene that are not recorded by the camera during a shot. An example in a script would be: "CU of Bill as we hear Sam slamming the door in the BG (O.S.)."

over-the-shoulder shot   A shot taken from the perspective of over an actor's shoulder. This type of shot entices the audience, making them feel as though they are a third party witnessing the scene. One actor might tell a secret to another actor during an over-the-shoulder shot. Or, perhaps a bedroom scene might be shot over the actors' shoulders to make the audience feel as though they are present. The shot is from a third-person point of view, so the audience isn't seeing it from either actor's perspective.

POV   Point of view; a shot approximating the perspective of an actor. In a script you might see, for instance, "The bracelet is shown from Paul's POV." You would be seeing the bracelet through Paul's eyes, viewing it from Paul's perspective.

reverse close-up   A close-up of the other actor once the initial actor's close-ups have been shot.

SFX   Special effects; graphics or sounds normally added after the actual shooting of a commercial. However, sometimes the effects are done at the time of shooting. For example, in a script you might see something like, "Jill is cooking over the stove as it blows up (SFX)."

shot   What is recorded by a single operation of the camera from the time it starts to the time it stops.

single shot   A shot that contains only one person or product.

SUPER   This abbreviation stands for "superimposition"—one image appears over another (much like a double exposure). In commercials, the term usually refers to words displayed over the recorded images. An example in a script would be: "SUPER: 'Coke adds life.'"

take   A single attempt to record a shot on camera. During the shooting of a commercial there will be many takes of a particular shot.

tight shot   A shot that is very close to its subject. This usually refers to an extreme close-up (ECU) or a close-up (CU). You might hear the director say to the cameraperson something like, "Let's tighten the shot," which means either the camera will move closer to the subject(s) or the cameraperson will zoom the lens closer.

two-shot   A shot that contains two subjects.

VO   Voice-over; words spoken off camera that accompany the images onscreen. In other words, the actor speaking is not on camera. An example in a script would be: "JANE (VO)."

wide shot   A shot covering a relatively large area of the set. This usually refers to a long shot (LS) and/or a master shot.

The Storyboard

Most commercial scripts are presented in the form of a storyboard. The storyboard is a cartoon drawing demonstrating how each shot will appear onscreen, much like a comic strip. Under each picture are written the words that will accompany the image. Storyboards aren't always available for the actor on every commercial audition, but if you are lucky enough to see one, study it carefully. It will give you the most accurate description of the type of image the auditioners are looking for. An example of a storyboard appears on the following pages.

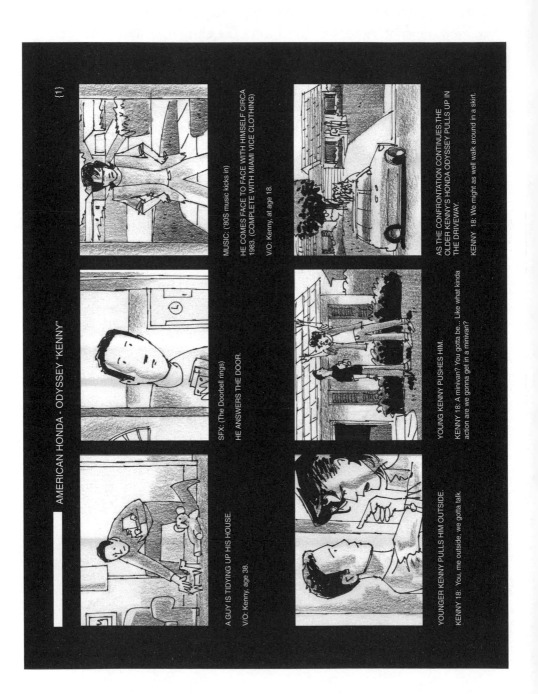

{1}

AMERICAN HONDA - ODYSSEY "KENNY"

A GUY IS TIDYING UP HIS HOUSE.

V/O: Kenny, age 38.

KENNY 18: You, me outside, we gotta talk.

SFX: (The Doorbell rings)

HE ANSWERS THE DOOR.

MUSIC: ('80S music kicks in)

HE COMES FACE TO FACE WITH HIMSELF CIRCA 1983. (COMPLETE WITH MIAMI VICE CLOTHING)

V/O: Kenny, at age 18.

YOUNGER KENNY PULLS HIM OUTSIDE.

YOUNG KENNY PUSHES HIM.

KENNY 18: A minivan? You gotta be... Like what kinda action are we gonna get in a minivan?

AS THE CONFRONTATION CONTINUES, THE OLDER KENNY'S HONDA ODYSSEY PULLS UP IN THE DRIVEWAY.

KENNY 18: We might as well walk around in a skirt.

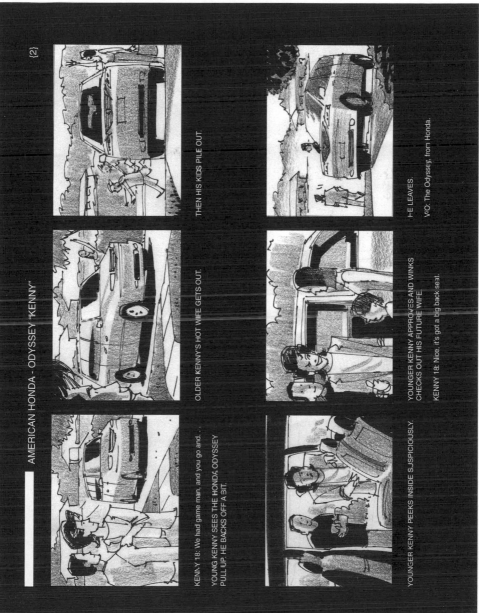

AMERICAN HONDA - ODYSSEY "KENNY"   {2}

KENNY 18: We had game man, and you go and. . .

YOUNG KENNY SEES THE HONDA ODYSSEY
PULL UP. HE BACKS OFF A BIT.

OLDER KENNY'S HOT WIFE GETS OUT.

THEN HIS KIDS PILE OUT.

YOUNGER KENNY PEEKS INSIDE SUSPICIOUSLY.

YOUNGER KENNY APPROVES AND WINKS
CHECKS OUT HIS FUTURE WIFE.

KENNY 18: Nice, it's got a big back seat.

HE LEAVES.

V/O: The Odyssey, from Honda.

How Commercials Are Shot

13

There are three basic types of shots: a close-up, a medium shot, and—like most acting careers—a long shot.

Many actors are under the impression that stage acting is much more difficult than acting for television shows, commercials, and feature films. This mistaken belief comes from the fact that stage actors think actors in the screen media can shoot a scene over and over again until they get it just right. They realize that stage actors don't have second chances, since they are performing in front of a live audience each performance.

What these misguided souls don't mention, or know about, are all the technicalities of acting for the camera. For instance, scenes are shot totally out of order; you don't have a month's rehearsal schedule as actors do for stage plays; and you have to hit marks and work in very small camera frames, which doesn't give you the freedom of movement and projection that you are permitted onstage.

Sequential Order of Shooting

Scenes in feature films, television shows (with the exception of sitcoms), and most likely commercials are shot out of order because it is the most economical way to get the job done. For instance, let's suppose you are shooting a commercial where the first scene takes place in the living room of a house. The second scene takes place at the local airport. The third scene takes place back in the living room, and the fourth back at the airport. Here's how we'd have to do it if we shot scenes in order. The crew would spend eight or so hours setting up the first living room scene and then, after completing it, strike the set, lights, cameras, and so forth, so the production trucks and crew could move all that equipment to the airport. At the airport they'd spend another eight hours or so parking dozens of vehicles and setting up for the second shot. Then, after completing this second scene, they'd move all that same equipment back to the living room, where they were just the day before, and spend another eight or so hours setting everything up just as it was previously. Then, after completing this third scene, the crew would have to haul everything back to the airport and go through the whole process yet again for the fourth and final scene.

A television show, feature film, or commercial could never be completed this way. Even if it could, it would be so costly that the production company would never recoup its investment. Wouldn't it just be easier to set everything up in the living room and shoot all the living room scenes while the production crew and sets were all in that locale? Then the crew could move to the airport, park dozens of vehicles, spend hours unpacking those vehicles, set up cameras and lights and so on, and shoot all the airport scenes while there. This cuts production time and costs to a fraction of what they would be if scenes were shot in sequential order.

You can see how complicated this could become in a feature film shoot. For example, let's say we're going to shoot all the living room scenes that take place in an entire film while we're in the living room, before going to a new location. In this case, you're going to spend five days in that living room shooting scenes 103, 158, 247, 128, 35, 85, 10, 27, 39, and 52. (Remember, scenes are not shot in order, hence the nonsequential numbering.) During the filming of each scene you'd have to remember what happened just before each scene and just after. Of course, you can look in your script, but I'm talking about how you felt emotionally.

For instance, let's suppose that we're shooting scene 127 today. In this particular scene, a husband and wife are getting out of their car and walking up to their house and opening the front door, all the while having an extremely heavy argument. Three weeks from now we're going to shoot scene 128, which continues from scene 127 and shows the couple entering the house and continuing their argument as they walk through the living room. And two weeks after that, we're going to shoot scene 126, which consists of the couple driving down a highway where the argument actually began.

When the actors shoot scene 127, they will have to think of how they're going to feel emotionally and with what intensity they're going to play the scene, since scene 128 will appear on the screen $\frac{1}{24}$ of a second later. And three weeks later, when the actors shoot scene 128, they'll have to remember the emotional intensity they used in scene 127, so that the performances match when they play on the screen. And of course, two weeks after that, when they shoot scene 126, they'll have to remember the emotional intensity with which they started scene 127—five weeks ago—since that's where they'll have to be at the end of scene 126.

Now, suppose that in this film your character is going bar-hopping and has to become more and more drunk between scenes 2,030 and 2,040. Today we're shooting scene 2,034, which means you have to be a little more drunk than you are supposed to be in scene 2,033, which we haven't shot yet, but a little less drunk than in scene 2,035, which we shot a month earlier.

When an actor tells you that stage acting is much more difficult than acting for the screen, he is more than likely showing his naiveté about the screen medium. I'm not suggesting that television and feature film acting is more difficult than stage acting; I'm just saying that they are so different, it's really hard to compare the two.

I have often heard acting instructors (especially those who come from the theater) say, "If you can act on the stage, you can act in the screen medium. Acting is acting, after all." Yeah? Well, using the same logic, if you can snow ski, then you can water ski. After all, skiing is skiing, right? *Wrong!*

Character Progression

One of the most difficult aspects of acting for the screen is keeping the character progression always going in the right direction. In other words, since feature films and television shows (with the possible exception of sitcoms) aren't shot in the order in which they unfold in the story, the actors have a "character progression" problem. A character in a play, feature film, or television show changes as he progresses through the script. The character isn't the same in the beginning of the show as he is at the end.

For example, maybe the female character is happily married at the beginning of this particular feature film. In the middle of the film, she goes through a messy divorce, and at the end of the film she is happily marrying someone else. Obviously, this character changes throughout the film. The actor in a play shouldn't have any problem with the character progression because every night of the performance, the progression is sequential.

However, in a feature film or television show (again, with the possible exception of a sitcom), the character progression jumps back and forth constantly throughout the filming. It is extremely difficult to keep track of what your character is doing and where in the progression your character is emotionally when you have literally hundreds of scenes to shoot. It can become as confusing as trying to keep all those Baldwin brothers straight.

The stage actor has a month or so of rehearsals. Generally, the first week he doesn't really have a "character" yet. He is searching for the direction in which he wants to take the character. The second week of stage rehearsals, the actor begins to "find" the character. Although not yet really developed, the character is at least starting to have some direction. By the third week the character is almost fully developed and is now taking on a life of its own. The fourth week is usually spent fine-tuning the character and adding nice touches to the portrayal.

However, in the screen media it would be extremely rare for you to have all this rehearsal time. In a feature film, for example, the character must be set from day one. The actor's portrayal of the character can't "grow" as he shoots the film, since the scenes aren't shot in sequential order. This causes many problems for actors and directors. Have you ever watched a film and thought to yourself, "I don't know . . . it just seems like a bunch of scenes thrown together"? Perhaps the character progression was off.

It is very possible that in a commercial shoot you will have some of the same problems—but to a much lesser degree, since for a commercial you're only shooting a few scenes at most. Television shows and feature films obviously take longer to shoot than they last on the screen. However, many actors, and the public in general, believe mistakenly that a thirty-second commercial takes, well, thirty seconds to shoot. And they believe that if the director does ten takes, then it should only take five minutes (thirty seconds per take) to shoot. *Wrong!* We spend anywhere from a day to an entire week shooting a thirty-second commercial. Most national commercials have much higher production values than the television shows they are sponsoring. After all, in reality the commercial is more important because it's what pays for the show (and our salaries) in the first place.

The "Shooting" Script

Keep in mind that by the time a commercial script gets to you, it has been debated, discussed, market-tested, then debated, discussed, market-tested, then debated, discussed, market-tested. . . . Clients are neurotics: people who worry about things that didn't happen in the past instead of worrying about things that won't happen in the future, like normal people. They spend a lot of time fretting over every single word in the script, so directors take this script very seriously.

Sometimes actors want to give us suggestions about how to improve the script. Don't do this! I've even had actors arrive on a set for an actual commercial shoot with a rewritten script that they want to "submit" to me. What these actors don't realize is that I can't make *any* script changes on the set without getting permission from dozens of people. And I could expose the client's company to a lawsuit just by changing a single word. Keep in mind that many attorneys have spent many hours going over this script to try and keep us from getting into any trouble over the content of the commercial.

So when you arrive on a set, be prepared to perform the commercial word for word as it's given to you. If there are any changes to be made, they will be made by the committee—and you know how long it takes the committee to make a decision!

Once you're on a set, assuming it's your first commercial shoot, you'll be surprised by how many people make up the crew. You won't believe how much equipment is present. It can be kind of intimidating, but keep in mind that we're there for you. We're on your side. We cast you, so obviously we must have complete faith in your ability to perform well on our set.

Your Relationship with the Crew

This should go without saying: *always behave professionally on a set!* I say "should" because, believe it or not, some actors don't. You wouldn't believe some of the behavior, much of it naughty, that I witness on sets. That's why you aren't allowed to have a nativity scene in Los Angeles. Not for religious reasons—it's just that no one can find three wise men and a virgin.

Be nice to everyone on a set. Keep in mind, though, that some people might not have your best interests at heart. Someone on a set may seem like a friend, but remember, a halo only has to fall ten inches to become a noose. Be aware of anyone who falls at your feet—he may be reaching for the corner of the rug. Everyone on a set has an agenda, so just mind your P's and Q's.

We realize this is your day to be a star, and most directors will treat you that way, whether we're shooting a commercial, a television show, or a feature film. However, the rest of the crew is not that impressed with you. Usually, for them it's not an "artistic" day. There are some creative positions on a crew, but many crew members are there for a day's work. Often it's just a job for them. Don't get me wrong. Crew members are generally very nice to actors. I'm just saying that people on sets are used to working with actors, usually very well-known ones, and aren't impressed with your position. So be humble and treat the crew with respect.

Believe it or not, crew members can make you look better or worse than you really do. I've seen it happen on more than a few occasions—for example, when I've been on a set looking at an actor and trying to figure out what's wrong with her face. Maybe there's an extra shadow under one of her eyes and I'm wondering, Who did her make-up—Bozo? Perhaps I'm looking at her and thinking, Nice dress—how many potatoes did it hold? Maybe I'm looking at her 'do and thinking, Does she dye her hair or is it naturally blue? Then later I'll find out that the make-up, hair, and wardrobe personnel didn't like that prima donna who wears the colored underwear that showed through her clothes and obtains her hair-care products from Petco. So perhaps they did their best that day to make her look permanently frightened.

Perhaps I'm looking at an actor who appears to look older on camera today than he did yesterday. He looked fine twenty-four hours ago, but now it appears as though bartenders should check his pulse instead of his ID. Then I'll find out that the actor had an argument with the first assistant cameraman, who pulls the focus. If the focus is too sharp, all the wrinkles show.

You can see the pattern here. The crew can help you or hurt you. You think these things don't happen? Then you're probably that type that thinks Eminem is a candy. Perhaps you should enroll in that Reality 101 course being taught at the local university.

Also, keep in mind that many directors don't know how to direct actors. Before becoming a screen director, I was a dialogue coach for some of the best-known top directors in Los Angeles. A dialogue coach is someone who helps the director get the performances he needs out of the actors. Many times I would get instructions from the director on what he wanted and then had the job of translating it to the actors and working on getting those desired results. This is one of the main things that prepared me to become a director.

Sometimes a screen director will be referred to as a "traffic cop." "Let's put a dolly track here—the actor walks left to right as we dolly the camera, right to left. . . ." The phrase comes from the fact that he's using his hands in a "traffic cop" way and, with his matter-of-fact direction, provides no emotional support for the actors and their characters.

I used to teach at the number one institution for directors and producers. It took me years to get them to let me teach a class for directors on how to direct an actor. The administration spent all its time teaching the technical facets of the business. In fact, very few schools for directors teach any classes in the art of directing actors. For some reason, they assume the actor will know his craft, and therefore the director can concentrate on all the technical problems that come up during shoots.

The point is, be prepared to give *yourself* a lot of character direction. Remember, the director has a jillion things to worry about on that set. You have but one—your acting.

The Actual Shoot

For sample purposes, let's use the following commercial to show how a commercial is shot:

> SON: Golly gee, Mom, my teeth have stains on them.
>
> MOM: Golly gee, son, I see what you mean.
>
> SON: Golly, Mom, what can I do about the stains?
>
> MOM: Gee, son, try using Presto 98 Teeth Cleaner.
>
> SON: Gee, Mom, you're the greatest.
>
> MOM: Gee, son, so is Presto 98 Teeth Cleaner!

This sample commercial script seems like a fairly simple one to shoot. There are only six lines, and one would assume that the actors would just stand next to each other and deliver their lines. You might think that such a commercial would be shot in less than fifteen minutes, tops. *Wrong!* This commercial could take an entire day, or even several days in actual production time, not to mention the weeks needed for post-production (editing, etc.). And this doesn't even take into account all the weeks of preparation it took to get a script everyone could agree upon.

Why should anybody make such a fuss over these few lines? In a stage play, a few lines go by so quickly that one can hardly remember them at the end of the show. But the few lines in the above commercial are the *entire* show. So the importance of those few lines consumes everyone involved.

Once you arrive on the set, you (along with the product) are the star. Make-up people, wardrobe personnel, hair stylists, and hundreds of other people are there to make you look good, and after a few rehearsals, they will be busily working on you. Generally, a set is a very actor-friendly place to be, especially in a commercial shoot, where you're not going to be working with the same people day in and day out over a few months or even years, as you would if you were doing a television series or feature film. But you still need to be alert as to who's a friend and who's a foe. Certain natural conflicts are set up in advance by the very nature of everyone's jobs. For instance, the client will probably be on the set. In fact, there will probably be more than one person representing the product, and they'll all have their own ideas about how this commercial should be shot.

When directing a feature film, I don't really have to worry about clients. It is accepted that the director is in control on the actual set. In a commercial shoot, though, there are a bunch of "chiefs." Yes, the director is in control; it's he from whom you take your direction, and he only. However, the client will usually be trying to filter information to the actors via the director about how he wants them to perform. It is considered in very poor taste, and is frowned upon by everyone involved, for clients to speak directly to the actors about how they want them to portray their characters and other such matters. If a client ever gives you direction on a set, you should consult with the director before making any changes to your performance.

Sometimes the client is upset with the director because he thinks the shoot is moving too slowly. The director of photography is upset with the director because he thinks the director is moving too quickly. The wardrobe people are upset either because they think the director is moving too slowly and their wardrobe isn't looking as good as it did early in the morning or because they think the director is moving too quickly and not giving them enough time for changes and last-minute primping. And the make-up people are upset either because they think the director is moving too quickly and not giving them time to make the actors look their best or because they think the director is moving too slowly and the make-up is beginning to run.

I could go on and on about these inherent conflicts. It is up to the director to set the pace and try to keep everyone happy on a set. These conflicts used to ruin my day, because I could scarcely believe how they crept into almost all commercial shoots. I guess I've reached that age where one learns to be amused rather than shocked. When I was young I was told, "You'll understand when you turn fifty." I am fifty and I don't understand a thing.

You want to stay out of any conflicts. Be careful about offering your opinion about them. Believe it or not, even with all these conflicts, you'll usually arrive on a set with a good feeling about what is taking place there. We're all there for the same reasons.

"Roll Camera"

When everything is set and ready to go, the director will turn to the assistant director and say something to the effect of "This one's for picture" or "Picture's up." This simply means that the director doesn't want any more rehearsals and is ready to actually roll the film or tape.

The assistant director then takes over the set, under the direction of the director, to start preparations for shooting the first take. The assistant director will then quiet everyone down by saying, "Settling." Often people continue to chatter quietly, and he will then say, "Settling, please," more forcefully. If the chatter continues, you don't want to know, nor can I put in print, what he yells next.

A moment later, the assistant director will say, "Roll sound." At this point the sound person starts his tape rolling as the cameraperson rolls the film or tape. A few seconds later the sound engineer will yell out, "Speed." This just means that the sound tape is now rolling at the correct speed and he is all set to go.

The second assistant cameraperson will then "slate" the commercial. He will call out, "Scene 22, take 4," for example, as he slams the two sticks together at the top of the slate. The slate contains the scene number, take number, director's and cameraperson's names, date, product name, and so on. This is important because when we get into the editing room, we need to know the take number and scene number of every shot. Otherwise it can become very confusing about which shots go with each scene, whose POV a particular shot was taken from, and so on. You can't imagine how many scenes in a television show or feature film we would be unable to identify if they weren't marked.

I'm not going to print every take. Many takes don't work, because of either technical problems or an actor's performance. Why don't we print bad takes? The main reason is, it's costly. So directors need a way to identify which takes they are going to actually have printed.

Think of our takes as a proof sheet of your still photography shots. It is much less expensive and more efficient for you to look at a proof sheet before deciding which photos to print and/or blow up. Film is expensive, so I'm only going to print good takes. For instance, at the end of a sequence of shots, I might turn to the script supervisor and say, "Print takes 4, 8, 9, and 12."

The reason the second assistant cameraperson slams those two sticks together in front of your face is so we can synchronize the picture with the sound. It's much more complicated than this, but, simply put, we feed in the piece of film that has the visual and match it up with the tape that has the audio. We match it so that when the stick comes down and hits the board, the sound will be heard. Therefore, we have put the two together precisely at the correct time so that the sound and picture will now be matched from that point forward. We have a much more sophisticated way of matching the sound and picture these days by time code. However, we still hit the sticks as a backup in case the timing is off on the time codes.

The slate is then taken out of the frame. Next, the director will call "Action," and that's when you're to begin your opening shots. After you have finished your dialogue and closing shots, the director will eventually yell "Cut." There is a sigh of relief from the actors when the director yells "Cut, that's a print," which means he liked that particular take.

After the director is satisfied that he has the perfect take, he will most likely do a "protection shot," which just means he wants to have an extra take in case something happens to the original one. For instance, the negative of the first take he liked could get scratched when the film is being developed. Perhaps we didn't notice the boom microphone barely hanging down into the frame during a particular take. Maybe a crew member's reflection can be seen in the mirror on the bathroom wall. There are a million reasons we might think a take looked good when we shot it, only to find out in the editing room that we needed a backup.

The Shots

Each scene will itself have constant cuts. For instance, first the director will shoot what is called the "master shot." This is an establishing shot to show who is in the scene. For example, let's say the commercial takes place in a living room where a mother and son are speaking to each other. The director will most likely shoot a wide shot of the room so that both characters are seen. We've now shown the audience who is in the scene and where the scene takes place, which sets the foundation for the action to follow.

Next, typically the director will move in for a tight two-shot. A two-shot is just that: a shot of two people. Their heads will fill the frame, with very little, if any, of the living room showing.

Next, the director will probably move in for the over-the-shoulder shots. We'll shoot Mom's first. In other words, the son will stand in his original position while the camera, which is behind his shoulder, is focused on Mom. We run through the complete dialogue again. Then we'll reverse the over-the-shoulder shot and focus in on the son. Mom will stand in her original position while we shoot over her shoulder, filming the son and his reactions. The actors again run through the same lines of dialogue.

Now we'll move in for the close-ups. First we'll shoot Mom's. The camera will be only on Mom, and we won't see the son at all during these takes. Sometimes, depending on the angle, the actor playing the son might be able to stand in his original position, but this is the exception. In many cases, the person being talked to for these takes cannot be in his original position because the camera will be there, as well as lights and other equipment.

In our example, the son will have to stand off camera, and Mom will have to look toward his original direction—where the camera is now. You will find that it can be very disconcerting even for just a few lines to direct your conversation in one direction when the person with whom you are speaking is not actually in that position. So practice!

Next, we'll shoot the son's close-ups. The shot is reversed (hence the term "reverse close-up"), with the mom over to one side and the

camera on the son. Again, these shots take hours to set up. Every time there is a change—for example, when a camera is moved to a different position—the whole set has to be re-lit, much equipment repositioned, and the like.

Notice that we have gone from wide shots to close-ups. It is very common to shoot this way. The most difficult lighting setups are usually the wider shots. So we spend the time lighting an entire area for the master or establishing shots and then slowly move in closer and closer. For example, in the above illustrations we moved from the master or establishing shot to the two-shot, then to the over-the-shoulder shots, and finally to the close-ups.

Of course many other shots can and probably will be shot. There will probably be at least a few POV shots. As mentioned in chapter 12, POV shots are shot from some point of view, usually that of an actor. For example, perhaps in our commercial Mom spots the product lying on a side table in the living room. Watch television shows, feature films, and commercials and you'll be amazed at how many POV shots you'll see.

We can also, for example, shoot a low and a high angle on the mom and the son, respectively. In other words, we might shoot slightly up at the mom and slightly down at the son. This could give Mom the look of superiority—which you'd want, since she's the one handling the product. Shooting up at someone tends to give that character the advantage, and shooting down at someone tends to put him in an inferior position. Next time you watch a television show or feature film, notice the angles. For instance, a husband and wife might be having an argument. Even though the husband may be taller than the wife, the director might decide to very subtly shoot down at the husband and up at the wife. This would perhaps give the audience the impression, psychologically, that the wife is winning this argument. You should watch the way shots are put together as they unfold onscreen; this awareness will help your performances in the future. Here we go again with that great tool for actors: observation.

We will do take after take. The reason we keep doing takes usually has nothing to do with your performance. We may make adjustments to it after each take, but generally we do more takes for technical reasons. Perhaps the dolly grip pushed the dolly or camera too far and missed the marks. Maybe an airplane flew overhead, or there was a rustling noise on the sound track from an actor's clothing rubbing up against the microphone. Maybe the assistant cameraperson missed a focus-pull. It's possible the boom guy lowered the boom into the top of the frame—and so on, and so on, and so on, and so on.

The point is, shooting a commercial can be a long, grueling day. I've only given you a thumbnail sketch of how the shooting takes place. And I was assuming that the commercial was being shot indoors. If it's to be shot outdoors, the process becomes even more complicated. I don't even want to go into all of the lighting problems an outdoor shoot entails. And keep in mind that the earth rotates, so the lighting is changing by the second! On shooting days I actually get a printout from NASA of the azimuth angle of the sun to the earth in one-minute increments for each day. I have to keep the lighting the same with regard to shadows and the like throughout the shooting of a particular scene. Since the scene most likely will take almost the entire day to shoot, the lighting has to appear as though the length of time used for the scene is the same as the length of time during which the scene would have naturally unfolded.

Remember that each setup (i.e., each different shot) takes many hours to arrange. The commercial may even be shot with many different variations and scripts. This means all of the above steps would probably have to be repeated for each variation of the script. Be prepared for hard work when you're cast in a commercial.

Then all those hours of work and rolls of film will be edited into a final product (or products) that will be shown to various audiences for testing. And after all the testing has been completed, the commercial might be re-edited again and again before being shown to the general public—if it ever is!

That's a Wrap   14

The greater danger for most of us is not that our aim
is too high and we miss it,
but that it's too low and we reach it.

You are on your way to becoming a
successful commercial actor. You now know the basics of what it takes
to make a commercial sound as though there is no script and the actor
is just expressing his true feelings about the product. You know how
to perform with a partner in an audition, and you know the basics of
how a commercial is shot. When it comes to your success as a commercial actor, you must aim high; it is no harder on your gun to shoot
the feathers off an eagle than to shoot the fur off a skunk.

But please don't kid yourself. This business is hard work. One of
the biggest problems with success is that the recipe for it is about the
same as that for a nervous breakdown. You can't depend on a rabbit's
foot for good luck—it didn't work so well for the rabbit. Luck is a
dividend of sweat—the more you sweat, the luckier you'll get. Yes,
there is some luck involved in success. However, when you get that
lucky break, you'd better be prepared for it. Continue to study your
acting craft. Luck is when preparation meets opportunity.

Be nice to everyone in this business. Someday that grip you treated
poorly might become a big producer. That production assistant who
brought you coffee might someday be the director of a feature film for
which you're auditioning. Everyone on a set is important to you, the
actor, not only as a fellow human being, but also as a person who is
trying to make your job easier. You can easily judge people's character

by how they treat those who can do nothing for them. When God sizes up a person, he puts the tape measure around the heart, not the head.

And I do believe in karma! People who complain that they don't get what they deserve should congratulate themselves. Life is never fair, and perhaps it's a good thing for most of us that it's not. If you're looking for a fair business, you should probably look elsewhere.

How an actor plays the game shows something of his character; how he loses shows all of it. There will be times when you're going to be unhappy while trying to make it in this industry. I don't care who the actor is, he's had lean times when things in his career just weren't going his way. Just when you think you'll be able to make both ends meet, someone will move the ends. That light you see at the end of the tunnel might turn out to be a train.

The road to success is almost always under construction, so during the hard times it's important to maintain a positive attitude. It might not solve all of your problems, but keep it up long enough and it will piss off enough people to make it worthwhile.

I know you read crazy things about people in this industry. Many times I've read an article in a supermarket rag about a particular star concerning an incident at which I was present and then tried to figure out how the writer came up with that slant. For example, when I was an actor, back before I was growing hair everywhere but my head, I was a guest star on a very popular TV series involving three women. Two weeks after the shoot, I read an article that went on and on about how two of the female stars had gotten into a fist fight. The article was even accompanied by a photograph, as proof of the fight, of a scar on the shoulder of one of the stars. Great story, except for the fact that the scar was from an accident in Hawaii in which the woman had slipped and cut herself on a lava rock.

You'll read many articles about the bad behavior of stars. There is bad behavior everywhere. It's just that people in this industry have their lives on very public exhibit. Yes, there are many divorces, for instance, in this business (as there are in all businesses). But even in Hollywood there are more marriages than divorces, proving that preachers can still outtalk lawyers.

The point is, people are people. You can find good and bad in people in every region of the world. People just like you are making it in the commercial acting field. So can you. Try never to doubt yourself and your abilities. We can see those doubts when you walk into an audition.

While trying to make it in this industry, keep your head high. Live each day as though it was your last—after all, someday it will be. Why grieve because all your dreams haven't come true? Neither have all your nightmares.

See you on the set!

About the Author

Tom Logan is a member of the Directors Guild of America, the Screen Actors Guild, the American Federation of Television and Radio Artists, and Actors' Equity Association.

His feature film directing credits include *Dream Trap* (which he also wrote), *Escape from Cuba* (which he also co-wrote), *Shakma, The Night Brings Charlie, Shoot, King's Ransom,* and *Smooth Operator.* All of these feature films are in worldwide release.

He has directed many television shows, network movies of the week, music videos, and hundreds of national and international com mercials. His television pilot directing credits (all of which have sold) include *Modern Miracles* (which he also wrote), *The Neon Tiki Tribe* (children's TV show, which he also wrote), *Working Title* for the CBC (which he also produced), and the nationally syndicated children's TV shows *What If* and *Kid Town Hall.* Early in his directing career he wrote, produced, and directed many episodes of the number-one-rated nationally syndicated TV show *Real Stories of the Highway Patrol.* He also directed many episodes of the very popular TV series *BloodHounds, Inc.,* starring Richard Thomas.

Tom has won two New Discovery Awards: the 1996 Best Director Award for Outstanding Achievement in Direction for *Escape from Cuba,* and the 1995 Producers' Choice Award for Outstanding Direction of a Television Variety Program for a live telecast of the 1995 Miss North America Pageant.

He is also the winner of the Golden Halo Award for the Most Outstanding Contribution to the Entertainment Industry for his contributions as an acting instructor for the studios and for his acting seminars. In addition, he won the Bronze Halo Award for Outstanding Contribution to the Entertainment Industry for authoring two top-selling books. Both awards are given annually by the Southern California Motion Picture Council.

Tom no longer acts, but prior to becoming a full-time screen director he starred, co-starred, or guest-starred in hundreds of prime-time TV series, feature films, and live stage productions from New York to Los Angeles, and in over one hundred national commercials. In addition, he has had recurring roles on three network daytime serials, including, for twelve years, *General Hospital*.

Early in his career, Tom was an acting coach for the studios, whose clients included top stars from all three major networks, Academy Award winners, top baseball and football players, rock stars, and other well-known celebrities. In Los Angeles, he simultaneously headed the TV and film acting departments at two of the world's most prestigious acting schools—the American Academy of Dramatic Arts/West (1981–89) and the American Film Institute (1980–89).

Tom has given his award-winning acting seminars in five countries and forty-seven states, mostly for the same clients, for the past thirty years. He holds a bachelor of arts (*cum laude,* Honor Roll, Dean's List) in theater arts from California State University.

He holds the highest airplane pilot rating one can obtain from the Federal Aviation Administration—Airline Transport Pilot. He owns a Piper Arrow and is an instrument-rated commercial pilot who, although he doesn't have time to teach flying, holds all the instructor ratings one can obtain from the FAA—CFI, CFII, MEI, BGI, and AGI.

Tom has two sons and lives in Southern California.